Mo Interesting
than your
TEACHER

Stuart Wright

black dog publishing
london uk

introduction

Detail is very important in school curriculums and is totally necessary in order to pass examinations. However, in your own time and under your own steam, it would be nice to 'broad brush' it a bit – wouldn't it?

I think it would be fair to say that you have to be interested in order to learn and when you're young, that's not always easy. You can't get away from the detail you have to study at school, college or university, but outside of that environment it's often difficult to find the time to read a whole textbook about something that just came to mind and got your curiosity juices flowing. More often than not, when you read a textbook or go onto the Internet in order to find something out about a serious subject, the information available has been written by one of those clever experts, scientists, archeologists, statisticians or whoever.

Why can't they write things down in layman's terms instead of blinding us all with science, and why don't they make it interesting? A few giggles woven in would also be nice from time to time but that's not the done thing and I don't understand why – do they do it on purpose? If you want to find something out, you don't always need to know and you don't always want to know every tiny detail. Sometimes it's nice to just understand the basics and then move on. That's fair enough isn't it? So, let's have a look at some un-waffled, bite sized chunks of interesting information without getting bored and bogged down in minute detail. You never know, you may be able to teach your teacher, tutor, husband, wife friends or parents something!

BAT

B

Manager of
speech
department

Camera
operator

The lens

Air
conditioning
plant

Screen

aste room

Department

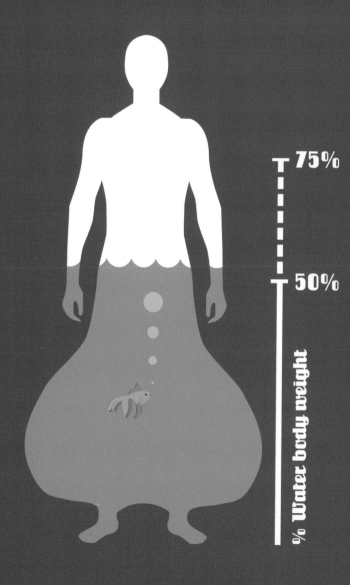

75%

50%

% Water body weight

THE WORLD
WATER RESEARCH

SUBJECT: BODY WATER

Figures vary slightly, but it is generally accepted that for people of average weight, water makes up between 50 per cent and 75 per cent of their body weight. In other words, on average, around two thirds of your body weight is water, which takes a bit of believing, but it is true. This can initially raise all kinds of questions to non-medically minded people, such as:

- Why does water not simply fall out of every orifice in your body?
- Why does it not drop down into your legs and feet, making you extremely fat and wobbly at the bottom, and very drawn and thin at the top?
- Why is it that when you stand on your head, you do not drown?

It may sound ridiculous, but just think about it for a moment. Two thirds of your body weight is water. Look at it this way: one litre of water weighs one kilogram or about 2.2 pounds, so if we take an average man, of say, 168 pounds, that means the weight of water in his body is about 112 pounds. So, again, if 2.2 pounds of water equates to one litre of water, this means the average man has the equivalent of around 51 litre bottles of water inside of him!

Where is all this water then? More than 70 per cent of your muscle and internal organ weight is water; your bones are around 22 per cent water; your body fat is around 14 per cent water. Even your skin is around 70 per cent water.

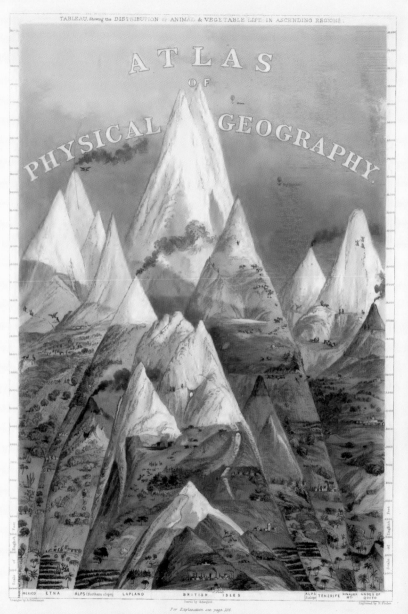

TABLEAU, showing the DISTRIBUTION of ANIMAL & VEGETABLE LIFE IN ASCENDING REGIONS.

ATLAS
OF
PHYSICAL GEOGRAPHY

MEXICO   ETNA   ALPS (Northern slope)   LAPLAND   BRITISH   ISLES   ALPS (S.slope)   TENERIFE   HIMALAYA M.ts   ANDES OF QUITO

Drawn by E. Weller.

Names by G.Musgrave.

Engraved by E. Fischer.

For Explanation see page 106.

LONDON. WILLIAM S. ORR & Cº

8

WHAT EXACTLY IS A MOUNTAIN?

21,171m

OLYMPUS MONS

8,848m

EVEREST

When is a mountain a proper mountain and when is it just a massive hill? Well, as it turns out, there is no universally accepted definition of a mountain. Explanations vary of what a mountain is, and here are just some of them:

A mountain is generally steeper than a hill.

A mountain is a land mass which projects well above its surroundings and higher than a hill.

A mountain is a large landform that stretches above the surrounding land of a limited area usually in the form of a peak.

A mountain is a natural elevation of the earth's surface, rising more or less abruptly from the surrounding level and attaining an altitude, which, relative to the adjacent elevations, is impressive or notable.

In the United States, a mountain is defined as "The highest point 1,000 feet or more above the base." This is one definition where an actual minimum height is used. However, it seems there are some landforms known as mountains in the US, which are less than 1,000 feet above the base, and yet they are still referred to as mountains!

Things get more confusing when you consider a height above sea level. If an island rises out of the sea to a height of 600 metres, the height of this mountain is 600 metres. If, on the other hand, a mountain rises 600 metres from a plateau, which is 500 metres above sea level, there are some people who would claim that this mountain is actually 1,100 metres high.

The highest mountain on earth is Mount Everest with an elevation of 8,848 metres. It is worth knowing though that there is a mountain three times taller than that on Mars. Its name is Olympus Mons, and it is 21,171 metres high. So to Martians, our tallest mountain would seem to just be a bit of a bump really.

METI

Methane is a major contributor to climate change. It is thought to equate to about 18 per cent of the total climate change contributors and is about 20 times more harmful to the environment than carbon dioxide. Around 60 per cent of methane produced on our planet comes from human activity, including fossil fuel production, biomass burning, animal livestock, manure management and waste management, of which almost half is produced by cows and sheep. Did you know that the average cow causes the same damage to the environment in one year as a standard car traveling 12,000 miles?

IANE

Do you know how many cows there are in the world?

1.3 billion

Do you know how many sheep there are in the world?

1.2 billion

Do you know how many pigs there are in the world?

2 billion

Between all the cows, sheep and pigs in the world, there is an awful lot of harmful methane produced. There are even reports that the amount of methane emitted by farm animals alone exceeds that of various combined industries.

So if car owners are taxed based on the emissions from their cars, why are farmers not taxed for their flatulent and belching animals? Believe it or not, taxing farmers for the methane output of their herds was actually considered by the New Zealand Government, but the idea was dropped after four hundred farmers with 20 tractors rallied outside parliament.

WHAT DOES A QUINTILLION LOOK LIKE?

Most of us have never even thought about such staggeringly huge numbers as a quintillion, but since the near collapse of the economy, millions, billions and trillions have become household words.

Most people know what a million looks like, and that is a one followed by six zeros.

Here is a look at the others.

ONE MILLION = 1,000,000

ONE BILLION = 1,000,000,000
—nine zeros

ONE TRILLION = 1,000,000,000,000
—12 zeros

ONE QUINTILLION =
1,000,000,000,000,000,000
—18 zeros

ONE SEXTILLION =
1,000,000,000,000,000,000,000
—21 zeros

ONE NONILLION = 1,000,000,000,000,000,
000,000,000,000,000
—30 zeros

ONE CENTILLION = 1,000,000,000,000,00
0,000,000,000,000,000,000,000,000,000,00
0,000,000,000,000,000,000,000,000,000,00
0,000,000,000,000,000,000,000,000,000,00
0,000,000,000,000,000,000,000,000,000,00
0,000,000,000,000,000,000,000,000,000,00
0,000,000,000,000,000,000,000,000,000,00
0,000,000,000,000,000,000,000,000,000,00
0,000,000,000,000,000,000,000,000,000,00
0,000,000,000,000,000,000,000,000,000,00
0,000,000,000,000,000,000
—303 zeros!

So, a billion is a thousand millions. A trillion is a million millions. A quintillion is a million, million, millions and a sextillion is ten thousand million million million. A nonillion is a million billion trillion quadrillion quintillion sextillion septillion octillion nonillion decillion, and a centillion—well, that is the biggest number ending in '-illion'!

ROSE COMB
BLACK BANTAMS

BLACK TAILED
JAPANESE
BANTAMS

POLISH
BANTAMS

WHITE
LEGHORNS

RHODE ISLAND
REDS

SILVER SPANGLED
HAMBURGS

BARRED
PLYMOUTH ROCKS

WHITE
PLYMOUTH ROCKS

PARTRIDGE
COCHINS

SILVER PENCILED
WYANDOTTES

CHICKEN EGGS

FRESH FROM THE NEST

All around the world, millions and millions of chicken eggs are eaten every day. But where do they all come from, and how are they made?

Like humans, female chickens produce their eggs through ovulation. However, unlike humans and other mammals, the eggs are automatically grown and laid by the chicken, without having to be fertilised first.

So, which bit of the egg grows first–is it the shell, the yoke or the white? Well, inside a hen are ovaries and oviducts–ducts leading from the ovaries. The ovaries have follicles and each one of these is a tiny egg, or yolk, waiting to be sent along the oviduct.

Once the follicle separates from the ovary and commences its journey, a clear jelly substance called albumen, which is (egg-white), is made, and forms around the yolk.

The egg then actually grows the shell around itself by a process similar to bone and seashell growth. Around the egg-white there is a membrane, and stuck to this membrane are points where columns of crystalline calcite form. This calcite is produced inside the hen, and sticks to the membrane, gradually building up to 100 per cent coverage. The shell does not harden until the egg comes close to the point of exit and is exposed to air; however, if the hen has not taken in enough vitamins and minerals, the shell will not harden.

Continued...

Inside the egg

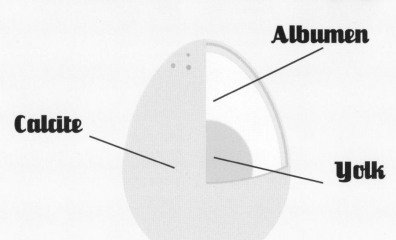

Albumen

Calcite

Yolk

Along the Oviduct

Which Comes First—The Hen or the Egg?

A popular question around the origin of chickens and their eggs is "which came first, the chicken or the egg?" Did some animal other than a chicken lay the first chicken egg, which contained the first chicken? If this were the case, the chicken egg would have come before the chicken. In reality however, many scientific theories suggest that this would not have been a simple event. For example, the theory of 'punctuated equilibrium' says that the actual starting of a new organism from its ancestral species is usually the result of very many mutations over time, combined with new geographical surroundings. This gradual mutation is known in the scientific community as cladogenesis.

If, however, one only considers eggs laid by chickens to be considered chicken eggs, then a reconsideration of the question "which came first; the chicken or the egg?" could suggest that the first chicken—which hatched from a non-chicken egg—laid the first chicken egg. In this case, the chicken would have come before the egg.

There is plenty of room for all of us on this planet

The world's population is presently at around seven billion people, and growing. So where do all these people live?

Asia: 60 per cent
Africa: 12 per cent
Europe: 11 per cent
North America: eight per cent
South America: five per cent

The most populous country in the world is China, with around 1.3 billion inhabitants. Not far behind is India, at 1.2 billion. The US comes third, with around a quarter of India's population, at roughly 311 million. 82 per cent of US citizens live in urban developments–that is, cities and suburbs–so this leaves vast parts of the countryside with hardly anyone living there. California and Texas are the most populated states, and New York City has the highest concentration of people in the country.

What about the United Kingdom? The population of the UK is currently about 62 million, coming 22nd in the world population stakes. In 1837–the year Queen Victoria took the throne–there were only five places in England and Wales with a population of more than 100,000 outside London. By 1891, this had risen to 23. Those figures are not only due to population explosion, but also due to people moving from the countryside to cities in order to find work.

Today, there are 66 places in the UK with a population of more than 100,000.

The world's population has grown at an absolutely astonishing rate. It was at around one billion in 1804, two billion in 1927, three billion in 1960, four billion in 1974, five billion in 1987, and six billion in 1999. It more than doubled in the last 50 years, and is predicted to reach between 7.5 and 10.5 billion by 2045–2050.

Is there enough room for us all? Well, three-quarters of the earth's surface is covered by oceans, and half of the land area is either desert (14 per cent), high mountains (27 per cent) or other less suitable terrain. Only about 10.5 per cent of the earth's surface is arable land, and only four per cent is habitable by humans; but even this four per cent is said to be under threat from rising sea levels, spreading deserts in China, Africa and Iran, and other environmental changes.

When you also consider that human consumption is said to have doubled over the last 30 years and is continuing to accelerate by 1.5 per cent a year, it is perhaps not surprising to hear that by some extreme estimates, humans will need to either stop consuming so many resources and drastically curb population growth or start within the next 100 years to colonise other planets.

... or is there?

DIPLOMATIC
IMMUNITY

Because diplomats represent their own government within foreign countries, there are certain safeguards that apply to their rights within their host country, which translate as 'diplomatic immunity'. For example, diplomatic communications are viewed as sacrosanct, and diplomats are allowed to carry documents across borders without being searched.

Diplomatic immunity is thought to have evolved during ancient times. It was not unusual in those days for messengers to be killed, depending on the news they brought. Legend has it that during the Greco-Persian War in the fifth century BC, King Darius the Great of Persia sent messengers to the Greek Spartans demanding "earth and water" which were symbols of submisson—and in response, the Spartans threw their messengers down a well.

Later civilisations began to respect the role of a messenger; it is an Islamic tradition that a messenger should never be harmed, even if they are the bearer of bad or insulting news. Within an official context, it was the British who first introduced diplomatic immunity to foreign ambassadors in 1709, its aim being to safeguard them against disagreements that could exist between foreign countries. The early arrangements were not always adhered to however–Napoleon infamously threw into prison those diplomats who he considered to be working against the French cause. Diplomatic rights were re-confirmed at the Congress of Vienna in 1814 and again at the Vienna convention on Diplomatic Relations in 1961. These diplomatic rules, protecting diplomats from being persecuted or prosecuted whilst on a diplomatic mission, are agreed upon and honored by virtually every country in the world.

In practical terms, this means that diplomats can drive as fast as they like, because they do not have to pay speeding fines; they can also accumulate large bills which they will never have to pay off, because they are exempt from the administrative juristriction of the host country.

But if a diplomat does commit a serious crime while in a host country, he may be declared as *persona non grata*, or 'unwanted person'. Such diplomats are then often tried for the crime in their homeland.

PARK WHERE YOU PLEASE

Average unpaid annual New York City parking violations per diplomat, November 1997 to November 2002

Country	Violations per diplomat	UN Mission diplomats in 1998
1. Kuwait	246.2	9
2. Egypt	139.6	24
3. Chad	124.3	2
4. Sudan	119.1	7
5. Bulgaria	117.5	6
6. Mozambique	110.7	5
7. Albania	84.5	3
8. Angola	81.7	9
9. Senegal	79.2	11
10. Pakistan	69.4	13

How far is the horizon, please?

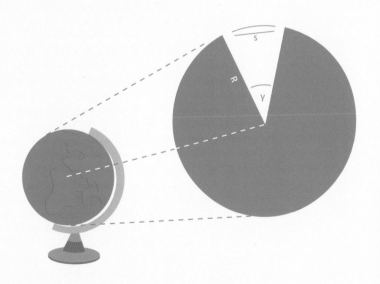

Have you ever seen ships on the horizon and thought, "I wonder how far away that is?".

Well, at first it may seem that the answer would be easy to work out, but in fact, a couple of solutions to this question exist, depending on where you are defining your measurements, as follows:

1. If you are defining the distance as a straight line between your eye and the horizon, then you take the height h of the level of your eye above the surface of the earth, and you then take the earth's radius as rp, into the following equation:

$$hs = h(2rp + h)$$

… and hs will give you the straight-line distance between your eye and the horizon.

2. You could also use the measurement from your feet, along the slightly curved distance along the planet's surface, to that point you can see on the horizon.

To work this out, draw a circle to represent the earth. Make one point on the circle representing where your feet are, and one point a little further round the circle, where the horizon is, and call the curved distance between these two points s. Next, draw a line from the point of your feet to the centre of the circle —along the radius R— and then another radius line from the horizon point to the centre of the circle. The angle between these two lines at the centre of the circle is the radian, and is called γ.

Now we use this equation to work out s:

$$s = R\gamma$$

then

$$\cos\gamma = \cos\frac{s}{R} = \frac{R}{R+H}$$

And solving for s gives:

$$s = R\cos^{-1}\frac{R}{R+H}$$

However, an approximate answer is relatively simple: if you stand at the water's edge on a beach, the horizon is about 3.24 miles away.

THE DRAKE EQUATION

Have you ever wondered what the likelihood is of ever meeting an alien? Well in 1961, Dr Frank Drake, Emeritus Professor of Astronomy and Astrophysics at the University of California, USA, produced an equation which allowed scientists to quantify the uncertainty of the factors that determine the number of extraterrestrials in the Milky Way with whom humans may come into contact at some point in time.

The equation he came up with looks like this:

$$N = R^* \times FP \times NE \times FL \times FI \times FC \times L$$

The equation takes into account such things as the number of civilisations in our galaxy with whom communication might be possible, the average rate of star formation per year, the fraction of those stars that have planets, and the average number of planets which can potentially support life.

Interpretations of common movements and gestures are as follows:

Locked ankles = Apprehension

Hand to cheek = Evaluation

Face turned away = Disbelief

Rubbing the eyes = Doubt and disbelief

Sitting, legs apart = Open, relaxed

Biting nails = Nervousness

Tilted head = Interest

Pinching bridge of nose, eyes closed = Negative evaluation

Scratching head = Thinking

Body Language

Body language is described as a term of communication using body movements or gestures instead of, or in addition to, verbal language. According to body language researchers, everyone sends and receives subconscious body language signals all of the time. They can take many forms, including blinking, body movement, facial expressions and even a slight movement of the eyebrows. Experts put the level of non-verbal communication at 80 per cent of all human communication.

It is important to remember, however, that no single body language sign is a reliable indicator. For example, consistent eye contact can indicate that a person is thinking positively about what the speaker is saying; but it can also mean that the other person does not trust the speaker enough to take his or her eyes off them. Similarly, one of the most powerful body language signals is said to be when a person crosses his or her arms across their chest; this is supposed to indicate that a person is putting up a barrier between themselves and others, yet it could also be that they are simply trying to keep warm.

How Do We Know the World is Round?

We are told that the world is round, but how can we be absolutely sure?

Many ancient cultures, such as the Egyptians, ancient China, and the Norse tribes, firmly believed that the earth was flat; they depicted it as a kind of disc or log floating on the sea.

Then the ancient Greeks put forward the idea of a spherical earth, most likely from the experience of travellers who observed the stars very closely and noticed how their altitude was different in other parts of the world.

In around 240 BC, one Greek mathematician, Eratosthenes, started studying the angle of the shadow cast by the sun when it was directly overhead on the longest day of the year, and comparing the size of the sun from two different places about 500 miles apart: Alexandria, and Syrene, which is much nearer the equator. He estimated

the angle as 1/50th of a circle; from that, he estimated the circumference of the earth.

Since then, astronauts and space probes have filmed the earth on numerous occasions and observed the size and shape of the earth from almost every angle. And we know that the only

geometric solid which looks like a circle from any direction is a sphere.

So how can we observe the fact that the world is round for ourselves? Well, there is the horizon—which you can never reach the end of, and over which thousands of ships sail every day and reach destinations beyond our view of the horizon. There are lunar eclipses, when the earth blocks the sun from the moon and casts a round shadow on the moon's surface. Then of course there are 24 hour time zones. When it is noon at one place on the earth's surface, it is midnight at another, and vice versa. If the earth was flat it could not possibly be noon and midnight at the same time.

But did you know that there are thousands and thousands of people who claim that the earth is indeed flat, that those ships that are lost at sea have in fact sailed off the edge of the earth, and that all the pictures ever taken from space are fakes? They have various theories, for example that the earth just stretches on horizontally forever. One theory is that not only is the earth completely flat, but that it is 5,592 miles deep. Another theory is that the North Pole is at the centre of our flat earth and Antarctica runs around the whole circumference of the earth. So, to travel around the World all you are doing is going round in a great big circle. Another theory is that earth is a disc shape and obviously is not perfectly flat, because there are hills and valleys. These people cannot use the word 'global' to describe anything, for obvious reasons.

tickling

Some people like being tickled and others do not. Many people break out into fits of laughter before tickling even commences.

It is generally accepted that there are two types of tickling. One is caused by a light movement over the surface of the skin and is called knismesis. This is, for instance, the sensation experienced if a fly lands on you or a spider crawls up your leg. Then we have what one could term the 'proper' tickle, which causes most of us to laugh our head off. This is known as gargalesis, where you can send someone into fits of hysteria by applying pressure with your fingers to a sensitive part of their body, such as under the arms or just above the knees. Gargalesis is said to be unique to primates, but some experts believe that rats can also be tickled.

So why is it that many of us fall about twitching and laughing like a deranged person when someone else tickles us, but we do not do the same if we perform the task ourselves?

There are a few theories on this, but the English naturalist Charles Darwin, who came up with the theory of evolution in 1859, gives us what is probably the best answer. He said that in order for tickling to be effective, a person must not know the exact point of stimulation in advance. In other words, if someone else is going to tickle you, it is the anticipation of not knowing exactly which part of your body they are going to make contact with that gives you the giggles. So if you tickle yourself, you know exactly where you will make contact and there is, therefore, no reason to laugh.

DO FISH GO TO SLEEP?

Whether fish go to sleep or not is a controversial subject. It is quite difficult to tell, mainly since fish have no eyelids; you may also come down in the middle of the night to find the fish in your aquarium happily swimming around as they do during the day. It seems that even many fish experts cannot entirely agree. The general consensus appears to be that most fish do not actually become unconscious like we do, but they go instead into a state of reduced awareness, rather like a very light doze.

Some fish go into a kind of hibernation in the winter months; during this time their metabolic rate slows down considerably. Their activity reduces, they stop feeding, go into a trance, and hover near the bottom of the lake or riverbed. Other fish bury themselves in mud and 'slow down' in this way, including a species of the Goby fish, which buries itself almost entirely, leaving only the tip of its tail touching the water above because, remarkably, it can breathe through its tail. One species—the Clown Loach—can play dead: when it feels a little tired, it drops to the bottom of the aquarium, rolls onto its side and looks completely and utterly dead. But, as with other fish, the slightest ripple in the water will disturb it and it springs back to life.

Boys & their Toys

Be it bikes, cars or lawnmowers, toys can bring an inordinate amount of pleasure to the average male. The singer and songwriter Rod Stewart, who has sold over 100 million records worldwide and is one of the best-selling artists of all time, holds his vast and lavishly detailed electric train set amongst his dearest possessions. The thousands of hours and many thousands of dollars Rod has spent on this pastime has led to his train set being featured on the cover of *Model Railroader* magazine, allegedly his proudest moment above and beyond singing in front of 50,000 people. For the super-rich male, however, a large dose of ostentation is more de rigeur. The family of the Sultan of Brunei are known for their extravagant purchases; the Sultan's younger brother became famous for his purchase of the largest luxury yacht in the world, at 525 feet (160 metres). The Sultan himself, as one of the richest people in the world is said to own:

✓ One Boeing 747 with gold-plated furniture, estimated to be worth around 233 million dollars

✓ Six smaller aeroplanes

✓ Two helicopters

✓ One theme park, called Jerudong Park in Brunei, which is worth three billion dollars.

The Sultan's car collection on its own can be said to be beyond the comprehension of most people. Reports vary on the exact figures, which are said to be in the region of 6,000 vehicles, of which:

367 Ferraris, 362 Bentleys, 20 Lamborghinis, 177 Jaguars, 130 Rolls-Royces, 160 Porches, 78 Aston Martins, 8 Maclarens, 531 Mercedes, 185 BMW's

... and many more.

It's been said that one of the reasons the Sultan has so many cars is that he cannot decide which colour he likes best, so he orders a few at a time in different colours.

35

36

Flies

Flies may be amongst the most annoying things on the planet, driving people to distraction. Flies will not take the hint. You can try to kill a fly hundreds of times but it will still keep coming back for more. Flies also have a reputation for being dirty, and the most basic facts about them prove that this reputation is not unfounded.

The fly most common to us is imaginatively called the house fly, for obvious reasons. It has six legs, can grow to around a quarter of an inch–6.35 millimetres–in length. Because flies have no teeth, their mouth has to absorb food like a sponge through a tube-shaped tongue, which they use like a straw. That presents no problem when they eat liquid food, but when they eat solids they have to turn it into liquid by vomiting on it. Flies are partial to wet rotten matter of various descriptions; however their favourite appears to be animal waste, because it has a very strong smell and is easy to find. I did warn you!

Maggots are unhatched fly larvae, and they do have their uses. Some doctors use maggots in hospitals to help wounds heal, because the maggots eat damaged flesh but leave the live flesh alone, speeding up the healing process. Anglers also use maggots to catch fish, and they are the most popular bait in European countries.

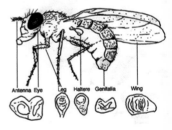

Antenna Eye   Leg   Haltere Genitalia   Wing

There are around 120,000 different species of flies throughout the world, living in and breeding in dustbins, rubbish tips, compost heaps and anywhere near animals; they are reported to travel up to 20 miles looking for food. 15 to 25 days after hatching from their larvae, they die.

The Pals Battalions

Great
Britain

France

Germany

Switzerland

Italy

Finland

Russia

Poland

Ukr.

Austria-Hungary

Serbia

Romania

Bulgaria

"YOUR COUNTRY NEEDS"
YOU

The twentieth century was shaped by two world altering wars. The Second World War, 1939–1945, has frequently been represented in films and television dramas, but the First World War, 1914–1918, is equally as important to remember.

It escalated very quickly, it was the deadliest war at that time in history, it was the first war where they used machine-guns, and the Second World War would never have happened without it. Especially frightening were the circumstances under which people were sent to fight, and the conditions in which they fought.

One particularly moving example of this rush to arms is the 'Pals Battalions'. When war broke out, the British Army was quite small, at around 450,000 men including reservists, which was nowhere near enough to defeat the enemy forces from Germany. After months of complicated tensions building up between European powers, Germany had invaded Belgium on 3 August 1914, a country that Britain was bound by treaty to defend. On realising his forces needed more men, the Secretary of State, Lord Kitchener, decided that rather than forcing men to join the army through conscription, they could be persuaded to sign up alongside their peers and friends. Kitchener started a campaign to get whole groups of local people from the same towns and villages to volunteer together with their pals; as such, the Pals Battalions were born.

There was mass euphoria in Britain. The expectation was that the Germans would be defeated quickly and that everyone would be home in a few months' time for Christmas. With Nationalism at a new height, men were queuing up outside recruitment offices and even lying about their age in order to join up and fight. Brothers, fathers, sons, cousins and workmates enlisted together, with many towns and cities unable to cope with the sheer number of volunteers.

The first Pals, from the Liverpool area, had signed up within just a few days, with sufficient volunteers for four battalions. Local pride kicked in and other areas quickly followed suit, keen to out-do neighbouring towns with a greater number of local volunteers. The relatively small town of Accrington in Lancashire had 1,000 volunteers in just over a week. There were sportsman's battalions, tramways battalions, public schoolboy's battalions and many, many more. Carried along on a wave of patriotism and peer pressure, one million men had volunteered by the end of the year.

What was making them sign up to fight? Well, many people at that time lived in extreme poverty and were struggling just to put food on the table. Great numbers of volunteers worked in mining and heavy industry; as you can imagine, these jobs were invariably dirty, exhausting and boring, with long hours as standard issue. Volunteering was seen as a great adventure and no-one knew

Opposing force movements

Allied force movements

Opposing Countries

Allied Countries

Soldiers Killed in the First World War

Germany	Russia
Austria	France
Turkey	British Empire
Bulgaria	Italy
	USA
	Romania
	Serbia

Total Casualties in the First World War

= 100,000 Allied Soldiers

= 100,000 Opposing Soldiers

what to expect. Just try to imagine yourself as a teenager living in those days, with very little money, very little food and in many cases, very little hope of any chance to travel. Most people would never have left the area where they were born. Suddenly, an opportunity raises its head for you to go abroad with your friends. You would get new clothes–uniforms–regular pay, regular meals, and the chance to see the world and defeat the Germans alongside your friends.

These men and boys walked proudly forward in their new uniforms into trench warfare that would bog down France, Britain and Germany for four long and torturous years. Unknown to those men signing up in the UK, massive casualties had already been seen by the French at Verdun, about 200 kilometres east of Paris. There were around 550,000 French and 430,000 German casualties. Recruitment still continued for 'the big push', which would take place on the Somme to help relieve the French forces.

The Battle of the Somme took place along a line of only about 32 kilometres. Artillery fire shot by the French and British was supposed to destroy the trenches dug by the Germans, from which they were firing. But often their artillery did not even destroy the barbed wire defences of the German trenches. The volunteers were ordered to march towards the enemy lines, and they were mown down indiscriminately. Within the first hour of the battle, 1,770 of the 2,000 Bradford Pals who advanced had been either killed or injured. On a single day, 584 of the 720 recruits of the Accrington Pals were casualties of war. The Leeds Pals lost 750 out of 900. Whole towns and villages lost many of their menfolk within a single 24 hour period as friends, relatives and workmates were sent up out of the trenches. They had no choice: if they did not run across the battlefield, shooting directly into enemy fire, they were shot by their own officers.

There were not many Pals left after the Battle of the Somme. They were either dead or badly injured. Many had limbs blown off and would be disabled for the rest of their lives. When someone died in those days the curtains in their house would be drawn. Within days of the beginning of the battle of the Somme there was hardly a house in many towns and cities that did not have its curtains drawn. As news of the continued carnage reached home, the volunteers slowed to a trickle, and the idea of Pals Battalions was eventually disbanded. It was too late for many of the towns and cities, as whole communities had been decimated by this idea of pals fighting together. Compulsory conscription, forcing people to sign up, was re-introduced in March 1916.

By the time the First World War ended in November 1918, 8.5 million people had been killed in total in combat. That is 2,396 times the capacity of the Titanic, or the entire population of Mexico City. The total casualties of mobilised men–that is people killed, wounded, missing, or taken as prisoners of war–was 37 million. That is enough people to fill the Titanic 10,431 times.

SNAKES

There are about 450 different kinds of venomous snakes on the planet. According to the World Health Organization, there are around 420,000 'envenomings' and 20,000 deaths every year from snake bites, but they also state that these figures could be much higher.

Amongst the deadliest snakes, in terms of the strength of their poison, are the krait, the taipan snake, the tiger snake, the beaked sea snake, the death adder and the fierce snake.

Here is an idea of the number of yearly fatalities across the world:

* The country with the highest yearly rate of deaths from snakebites is India, where there are estimated to be 10,000 to 12,000 annually, from Indian cobras, Russell's vipers, and saw-scaled vipers.

* South America sees around 2,000 deaths annually from pit vipers, rattlesnakes and coral snakes.

* Africa comes third, with puff adders, saw-scaled vipers and Egyptian cobras killing about 1,000 people a year.

* In Europe, ten to 15 people die every year, mostly from sand viper bites.

* Fourth is North America, where ten to 12 people die from bites from western and eastern diamond-backed rattlesnakes.

* Australia comes last, with two to four annual deaths from tiger snakes and eastern brown snakes.

Continued...

ANATOMY OF A SNAKE

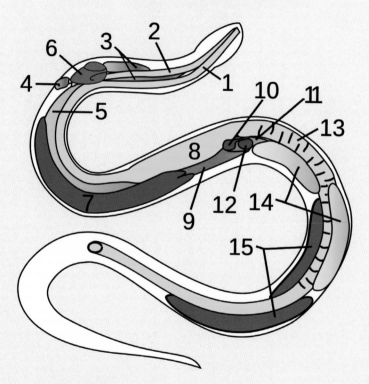

1	Esophagus	**9**	Air sac
2	Trachea	**10**	Gallbladder
3	Tracheal lungs	**11**	Pancreas
4	Rudimentary left lung	**12**	Spleen
5	Right lung	**13**	Intestine
6	Heart	**14**	Testicles
7	Liver	**15**	Kidneys
8	Stomach		

The most venomous snakes are by no means the largest ones. If you are talking about length, the Asiatic reticulated python, commonly referred to as the 'King of the Snakes', can grow up to 33 feet or ten metres in length. However, despite being shorter in length than the python—at an average of 20 feet, or six metres—anacondas are in fact accepted as the largest snakes because of their sheer bulk. They have an average girth of 30 centimetres, or 12 inches, and in the South American jungles they can easily grow as large in girth as a grown man.

Another one of the world's largest snakes, renowned for its hunting abilities, is the boa constrictor—a member of the anaconda family, which does not in fact need to be poisonous. Boa constrictors have hooked teeth with which to grab and hold their victim, whilst wrapping their muscular bodies around them, squeezing until dead. They have massive jaws, and often eat their prey whole, with their favourite choice of catch being monkeys, wild pigs, deer and the occasional jaguar.

Meal Deal
$4.99

Extra Chocolate!

Extra Cream

Chocolate Sundae

A calorie is the amount of energy or heat it takes to raise the temperature of one gram of water by one degree Celsius.

One calorie is equal to 4.184 joules, and a joule is a unit of energy used in science.

The calories quoted on food packaging are usually kilo-calories—kcals—and one kcal is equal to 1,000 calories.

So, a calorie as we understand it, is not actually a calorie at all, it is a kilocalorie.

Therefore, an item of food which is stated as having 300 food calories (kcals), actually contains 300,000 regular proper calories.

The calories in five pounds of spaghetti contain enough energy to brew a pot of coffee.

The calories in one piece of cherry cheesecake contain enough energy to light a bulb for an hour and a half.

217 Big Macs contain enough energy to drive a car 88 miles.

Breakfast ☆ Lunch ☆ Dinner

Open 7.30am to 8.30pm Daily

THE MYSTERY TERROR

FACT OR FICTION?
YOU DECIDE!

COMING TO A PLANET NEAR YOU

STARRING:

SOVIETY UNIONIO SOVIETA MAFIAN AND TERRORISTO

RED MERCURY

If red mercury does exist, it is incredibly scary—probably the most dangerous threat to mankind at this moment in time. However, if it does not exist, it has to go down as one of the biggest cons in the history of the world. Confused? It seems many other people are confused as well, including many physicists. Some strongly believe that red mercury does exist and take the threat very seriously, whilst others claim it would be impossible to make such a substance.

The red mercury stories began after the fall of the Soviet Union during the 1990s, when rumour had it that the Soviets had developed a substance which could be used to make a nuclear bomb in a relatively easy and cheap way. If that is not scary enough, it was also alleged that nuclear bombs made from red mercury could be manufactured to virtually any size down to that of an apple, and that the Soviet mafia had sold some of this substance to persons unknown. Stories still abound about businessmen hawking red mercury around the world and that certain unscrupulous individuals and organisations are prepared to pay almost anything in order to get their hands on it—even though they have no idea exactly what it is. These people are buying into a rumour, but if you happen to be a despot or a terrorist seeking nuclear capability, this kind of thing is right up your street.

Then again, there are those who claim that the whole thing is a massive scheme of disinformation. Government agencies state that the material known as red mercury does not exist, and that the myth was perpetuated in order to create a series of carefully planned stings to lure potential bombers in for capture by the authorities.

LOST TREASURE

The first thing most people think of when it comes to lost treasure is pirates.

The infamous plunderer Captain Kidd is a good starting point; since the 1600s there have been many stories about treasures buried by him. William Kidd was born in Scotland in 1645, and after failing to secure a commission with the British Navy, he took a privateer's license from the King allowing him to attack and capture French and Pirate ships, and split the proceeds with the government. However, this agreement did not last very long, and Kidd started to attack just about any ship containing valuables, officially making him a pirate himself.

Kidd was eventually arrested, and shortly afterwards some of his gold and treasure worth around $16,000—an absolute fortune at the time—was dug up on Gardiners Island, New York. Kidd tried to bargain for his life with promises of the locations of further treasures, but they were never revealed—and there has been a never-ending search for them ever since.

Probably the greatest and most elusive treasure in the history of the world is the Holy Grail. This vessel is rumoured to be the goblet that Jesus drank wine from together with his disciples at the Last Supper. Legend has it that this cup holds very special powers and there are many accounts as to where it could be located, if indeed it exists at all. The Saint Mary of Valencia Cathedral claims to have the Holy Grail already, but experts believe this to be a replica. There is also a story that St Peter carried it to Rome from where it was transported to a monastery in Huesca, Spain, for safekeeping during the Islamic invasions.

The Knights Templar—an early military order formed during the Crusades and endorsed by the Church—are also said to have had possession of the Grail at one point. These soldiers plundered gold, religious artefacts and anything else of great value from all over Europe and beyond. The story goes that when they were dissolved, some of the Templars were thought to have escaped and landed in Nova Scotia, Canada, and buried the Grail in what became known in folklore as 'the Money Pit'. Treasure hunters have already found a series of tunnels and flagged platforms, but the treasure unearthed to date only includes a few gold chains.

There is another lost treasure associated with one of the most notorious pair of robbers in the American West: Butch Cassidy and the Sundance Kid. After a series of bank and train robberies, these two were forced into one last heist. After robbing the Winnemucca Bank in Nevada, they had originally intended

Continued...

to head for South America by ship. But they then reconsidered whether they should take with them all the gold coins that they had stolen from Winnemucca Bank; Butch preferred paper money and securities because they were easier to carry. So they decided to stash the coins and rob paper money from elsewhere.

Together with their gang, Butch Cassidy and the Sundance Kid robbed a train carrying paper money, and then fled to New York and on to Buenos Aires, leaving the rest of the gang with their share of the paper money and the gold coins. It is thought that the gang then buried the $32,000 worth of gold coins next to a creek along the Stage Road near Wallace, Idaho—but these have never been found. At today's value they would be worth an absolute fortune.

During the Third Reich, the Nazis plundered masterpiece paintings, sculptures, gold, money and many other valuables from the countries they invaded in the Second World War. They also stole fortunes from individuals, many of whom were Jewish. The Dachau treasure is a huge collection of those fortunes, said to have been worth around $50 million, consisting of jewels and gold confiscated from victims of the Dachau Concentration Camp near Munich. The story goes that when the Allied forces were nearing the camp to liberate it towards the end of the Second World War, a group of SS officials made away with the treasure and escaped through the Austrian Alps using a route passing one of the lakes near Strasburg. The treasure is said to be buried in this area. After the war was over, a condemned SS Officer described the location of the treasure to a Dr Wilhelm Gross, an Austrian-born physician. He, in turn, later shared the information with an American Intelligence Officer called Greger and they both tried to recreate the route, which took them to Lake Lünersee, on the Austrian-Swiss border. Unfortunately for them, by the time they reached the place where the treasure was supposed to be buried, a dam had been constructed, submerging the area under about 75 feet of water. 1990 saw the dam temporarily emptied, so Greger returned, but he never found the treasure as it is thought that the weight of the heavy boxes must have taken them to the bottom and buried themselves in silt and mud. By all accounts, it must still be sitting there.

Captain James Cook was an explorer of the seas and discoverer of Australia for the Western world; he is also associated with a vast treasure, buried somewhere on a Hawaiian island, a story passed down through generations of Hawaiian natives. Cook is known to have explored the islands around 1778, and was killed there by the natives who took everything from his ship, including the treasure. The story goes that the King of the islands at that time did not understand what these objects were and took them to be magical, so he buried them. The island of Kauai has very high cliffs, is difficult to approach, and it is here where the treasure is supposed to be buried—but nobody really knows.

It is believed that if Cook's treasure could be found, then its value today would be beyond comprehension.

In order to illustrate the fact that treasure is sometimes found closer to

home, I must tell you about the 824 gold coins, or 'staters', that were found buried in a pot near the village of Wickham Market, Suffolk, UK, in 1992 by someone using a common metal detector. On examination, it was established that all of these gold coins were probably minted between 40 BC and 15 AD, shortly before Queen Boudicca led the uprising against the occupying Romans. The value of the coins at that time is estimated to have been between £500,000 and £1,000,000—that is $800,000 to $1.6 million—which still is an absolute fortune. This find is apparently the largest collection of Iron Age gold coins found in Britain since 1849, when a farm worker unearthed between 800 and 2,000 gold staters in a field near Milton Keynes.

WHY IS IT COLDER NEARER TO THE SUN?

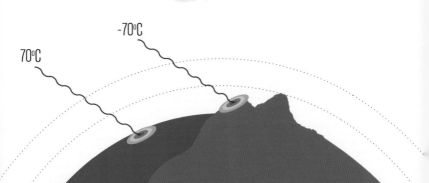

-70°C

70°C

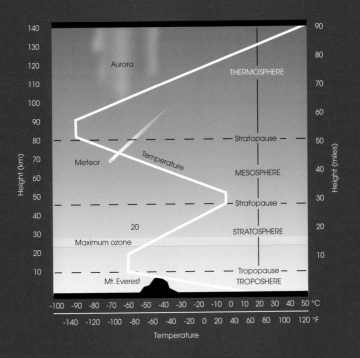

The sun is constantly throwing out intense heat, yet if you are in a plane—and therefore closer to the sun—and you are given the outside temperature, it is usually well into minus figures, depending on your altitude. Similarly, anyone who climbs a high mountain without the proper protective clothing on will die from hypothermia fairly quickly.

But why is this? If you are nearer to the sun whilst at the top of a mountain, then surely it should be hotter up there? Well, the sun's heat warms virtually all of our land, lakes and seas; but it passes through our air almost as though it is not there, and hardly heats it at all. Once absorbed by the earth's surface, this heat in turn heats the air next to it. As such, the higher you get, the colder it gets, because you are further away from the surface of the Earth that has been warmed by the sun's rays.

As you get further away from the overall surface of the Earth, it is reckoned that temperature falls by about 5.5 degrees Centigrade (9.9 degrees Fahrenheit) for every 1,000 metres' increase in altitude.

PLANET ⊕ POST

METEORITES!!!

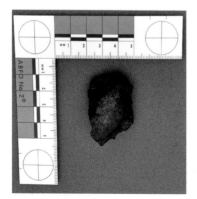

A meteorite is a stone or solid object that falls to earth from space. Prior to hitting the Earth's atmosphere it is called a meteoroid, but once it enters the Earth's atmosphere it becomes a meteor—also known as a shooting star. A meteor gets incredibly hot very quickly due to the friction in the atmosphere. Believe it or not, most of the shooting stars that you may see in the clear night sky are only as big as a small stone, but their glow gives them a much bigger appearance. The vast majority of meteors burn up entirely in our atmosphere; but if they do survive and hit the ground, they become known as meteorites. In other words—and thankfully for those whose houses may be standing in their way—very few meteors become meteorites.

It is widely believed that the dinosaurs were wiped out by an enormous meteorite around 65 million years ago. This thing is thought to have been a few miles in diameter, and made a crater in modern-day Mexico nearly 125 miles across and over half a mile deep. As a result, huge amounts of

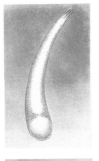

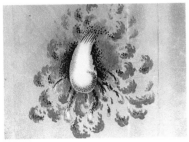

dust and debris would have filled the sky for years, blocking out the sun and killing most plant life. Fortunately, it is reckoned that a meteorite of that size is only likely to hit the Earth every 100 million years.

As you are reading this, there are astronomers and scientists looking into the sky and trying to detect space objects that might be on a collision course with us. One cannot help wondering how much warning we would have if they saw one tonight.

The chances of being hit by a meteorite are miniscule; but there is the curious case of a man in Bosnia who appears to be a little unlucky in this department, since his house has been hit not only once, but five times by meteorites. All five rock specimens have been examined by Belgrade University, who have confirmed that they are indeed genuine meteorites. They are investigating magnetic fields in order to see if his house location is in some way particularly attractive to meteorites falling through the atmosphere. Meanwhile, and perhaps not surprisingly, this individual has had his roof reinforced. He came to believe that he may have done something to offend some extraterrestrial beings, and that they are targeting his house

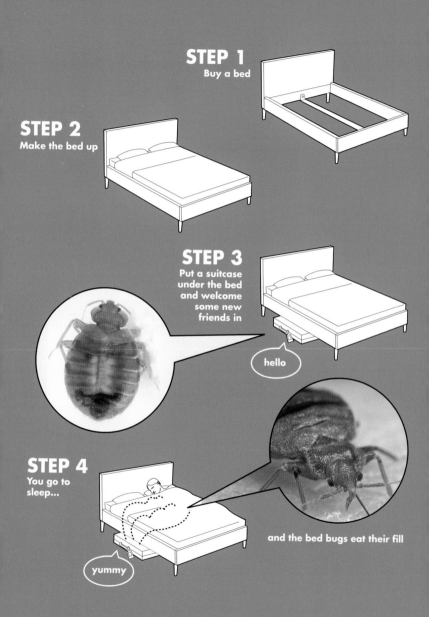

THE BUGS IN YOUR BED

Some people are frightened to death of bugs of any kind, but they may in fact be surrounded by them and even sleep with them without realising—because bed bugs and dust mites are far more common than you may think.

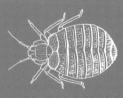

The kind of bed bug generally found in our homes is known as the common bed bug. Fully-grown common bed bugs are between three and five millimetres in length, with six legs and two antennae. They are brown in colour, oval in shape, and fairly flat—but their colour turns from brown to a reddish-purple after their meals of blood, and they become more rounded in shape because they are full.

Common bed bugs only come out at night, and they are adept at finding dark places to live within our homes. They huddle together within mirrors, pictures, mattresses, bed bases, headboards, plug sockets, telephones; just about anywhere you care to think of. They will stow away in any little hole they can find, such as in cracks, behind skirting boards and inside suspended ceilings. With regular meals, they can live for up to around 18 months. It takes around 18 weeks for a bed bug to become an adult, and a female can lay over 300 eggs in her life. These horrible little creepy crawly things can usually be detected by blood spotting and brown excrement spots on bedding, very tiny off-white eggs and, if there are a lot of them, a sweet almond-like smell.

Because they feed on blood, bed bugs never travel very far from the people they feed on. They are commonly picked up in hotel rooms, where they may also climb into peoples' luggage and become permanent residents. They are not known to carry diseases.

Next, and virtually impossible to detect at around 0.3 millimetres in length, are dust mites. Dust mites are also sometimes referred to as pillow mites or bed mites, and with their eight legs, they are in fact related to spiders and ticks. Since they live off particles of dead skin, they are commonly found living in beds, where humans spend around one third of their lives, shedding around one-fifth of an ounce of dead skin every week. It is estimated that dust mite excrement makes up around ten per cent of the weight of the average two-year-old pillow.

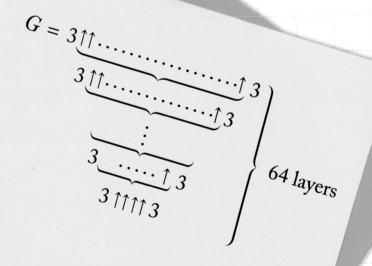

$$G = 3 \underbrace{\uparrow\uparrow\cdots\cdots\cdots\cdots\cdots\cdots\uparrow}_{\underbrace{3\uparrow\uparrow\cdots\cdots\cdots\cdots\cdots\uparrow 3}_{\vdots}} 3 \left.\vphantom{\begin{matrix} \\ \\ \\ \\ \\ \\ \end{matrix}}\right\} \text{64 layers}$$

$$3\underbrace{\cdots\cdots\uparrow}_{3\uparrow\uparrow\uparrow\uparrow 3} 3$$

60

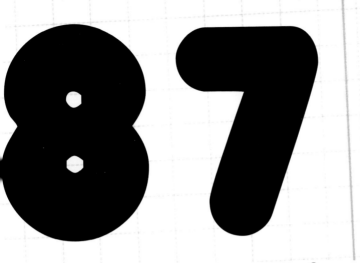

WHAT IS THE LARGEST NUMBER?

Most mathematicians will say that there is no such thing as the largest number. But we do have something known as "Graham's number", which is so massive that it holds the record for being the largest number ever used in serious mathematics. Graham's Number was invented by the American Ronald Graham—a juggler and acrobat as well as a mathematician—and it is the biggest number ever used in a proof. It cannot even be described with conventional numerical techniques, and is so big that there is not room within the observable universe to either write or digitally represent it.

What use would such a massive figure as Graham's Number be? Well, it was devised within a branch of mathematics called "combinatrics", which is used in computer science and statistical physics, where you might deal with large populations, making approximations and solving physical problems.

The combinatorics question that Ronald Graham answered in coming up with Graham's Number is as follows: "Take any number of people, list every possible committee that can be formed from them, and consider every possible pair of committees. How many people must be in the original group so that no matter how the assignments are made, there will be four committees in which all up, and all the people belong to an even number of committees?"

While we cannot show here the unthinkably large numerical answer to this question, we can reveal that the last ten digits of Graham's number are 2464195387.

Oil must be one of the dirtiest, smelliest substances on the planet, but it is also one of the most desirable. Because it has so many uses, it is not far behind gold and diamonds in the desirability stakes.

We all pull into a filling station from time to time to fill the car up, without giving it a second thought; but how does the fuel get there in the first place? Most of us have heard of oil refining, but what is that exactly—a big old boiling pot full of oil?

In very simple layman's terms, this is what happens. Once the crude oil has been extracted from the ground, it has to be cleaned of foreign bodies, such as sand and water. It is then heated and pumped into a tower, where it is exposed to very high temperatures; this chemically splits the crude oil to extract the various derivatives that become the oil products we know. This process is called 'cracking'. Petrol can be boiled out at only 40 degrees Celsius, but it can take over 400 degrees Celsius for heavy gas oil. Once heated sufficiently, the products are sat in the tower with the lightest products at the top running down in bands, to the heaviest products in the bottom. There are collection points located at intervals up the tower, which take away and collect the individual products according to their density. These are then ready for sale, apart from the residual, which has to go through further refining.

So the idea of a big old boiling pot is not so far off after all. However, these particular boiling pots would set you back between four and six billion dollars each.

GAS

NAPTHA
raw materials for chemicals & plastics

GASOLINE/PETROL

KEROSINE/AVIATION FUEL

GAS OIL/DIESEL

LUBRICATING OILS

HEAVY GAS OIL

RESIDUAL

LONDON COUNTY COUNCIL

MAIN DRAINAGE

MAIN, INTERCEPTING, STORM RELIEF,
AND OUTFALL SEWERS,
PUMPING STATIONS AND OUTFALL WORK

NOVEMBER 1932

REPAIRING THE FLEET SEWER.

SEWAGE

Some estimates claim that the UK creates around one and a half million tonnes of sewage per year–that is around the weight of one million hatchback cars. In the US, around eight million tonnes is produced per year.

What happens to all this sewage depends on where you live. In many countries where agriculture and farming is a massive part of the economy, raw sewage is spread onto fields as a matter of course. One international source reckons that more than 200 million farmers worldwide put raw sewage onto their crops. For instance, raw sewage in Pakistan fertilises about a quarter of the country's vegetables.

Most of us know that whatever goes down the toilet goes to the sewage works; but what actually happens to it once it gets there?

It is a complex process, so to summarise: raw sewage is filtered first of all in order to get rid of foreign bodies such as nappies and sharps. The next step is to put the refined sewage through a tank containing good bacteria that feed on it. The remaining sludge is heated at high temperature in order to kill any remaining toxins and we finish up with manure, about two-thirds of which is scattered back onto fields growing crops, and these crops are eventually sold in our supermarkets.

People say that some of the drinking water in large cities such as London has been recycled up to five times. It is true that a tiny proportion of tap water comes from the sewage treatment process. 80 per cent of London's tap water comes from the River Thames and the River Lee, with the remaining 20 per cent from groundwater–and some of the flow in the rivers gets there from sewage treatment works. Once it leaves the sewage treatment process, water is then put through natural purification in raw water storage reservoirs, before it blends with other water that eventually reaches rivers.

As for the water that is extracted from rivers for drinking water, this goes through a number of procedures such as filtration through sand, lava systems and UV-radiation, and plant systems, such as treatment ponds and constructed wetlands. After filtration, the water is disinfected, and thoroughly tested to ensure that it is safe to drink.

WHAT IS A BLOOD FACTORY?

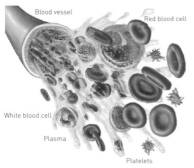

Blood vessel
Red blood cell
White blood cell
Plasma
Platelets

We are all blood factories. The average person has around five litres–8.79 Imperial or 10.55 US pints–of blood circulating around their body. There are three kinds of cells in our blood: red cells, white cells and platelets. All three types of cell are suspended in plasma and the split is approximately 55 per cent plasma and 45 per cent blood cells. The red cells carry oxygen throughout our bodies and remove carbon dioxide, and the white cells help our bodies to fight infection. The platelets, which have a sticky surface, form clots at a wound to stop us from bleeding to death. The carrier, plasma, is about 90 per cent water. Plasma has another function–apart from carrying blood cells, it also carries nutrients, hormones and proteins throughout our bodies.

So blood is very clever stuff. It is continually being manufactured within our bone marrow, which is the soft material in the cavities of our bones. Once manufactured, the blood is pumped by your heart throughout your body, carrying with it oxygen and nutrients from the food we have eaten and digested.

Your blood also carries carbon dioxide–which is a waste product produced by your cells of the metabolism process–from your tissues through to your lungs, where exhaled in your breath.

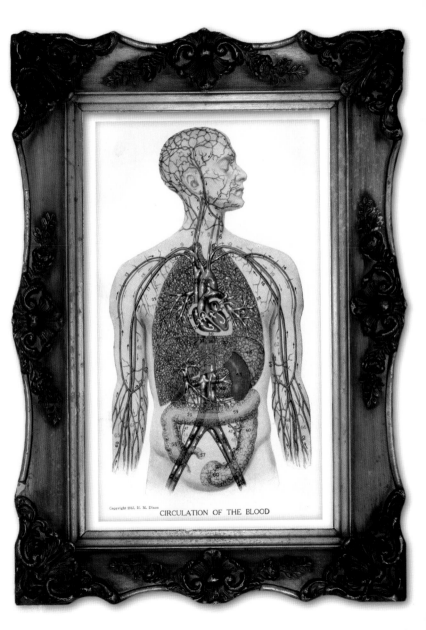

Copyright 1912, H. M. Dixon   CIRCULATION OF THE BLOOD

67

A handmade kilt takes about 15 hours to complete.

The oldest tartan is the Falkirk tartan, which dates to around 260 AD.

More than 4,000 different tartans are known to exist.

The average kilt is made of eight yards of material.

A woolen kilt weighs around 4.5 to 5 pounds.

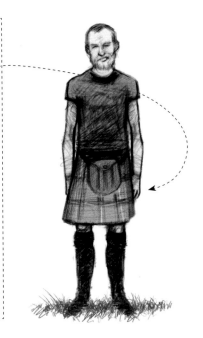

The four most popular tartans are the Black Watch, Stewart Dress, Dress Gordon and the Flower of Scotland.

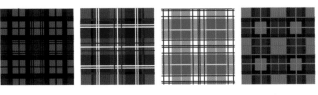

| Black Watch | Stewart Dress | Dress Gordan | Flower of Scotland |

Kilts

Because kilts are associated almost exclusively with Scotland, it comes as something of a surprise to learn that the person widely credited with inventing the modern kilt was Thomas Rawlinson–a Quaker entrepreneur from Lancashire in the North of England in around 1727.

At that time in Scotland, most men wore a Breacan an Fheilidh, or belted plaid. This was a length of thick woollen cloth up to 6.4 metres in length and about a metre and a half wide, made up from two loom widths sewn together. Underneath this, a full-sleeved garment stopping below the waist was worn, known as a leine. In harsh weather, the belted plaid could be brought up over the shoulders or head for protection; it could also be used as a camping blanket.

The story goes that when Rawlinson came to Inverness to establish an iron works, he noticed that the belted plaid worn by workers could be made more comfortable for the kind of physical work involved in producing iron, he took the garment to a tailor, who responded by cutting it in two. Rawlinson introduced this new garment amongst his workers and apparently liked it so much that he began to wear it himself. Since this story became popular however, illustrations from before 1727 have come to light of people wearing simplified kilt-like garments on only their lower halves, so it may be that Rawlinson just saw this garment elsewhere and introduced it to his workers.

A twist to the tale comes in with the Austrians, who now believe they invented tartan, since a discovery was made of a fragment of material found in a peat bog in Molzbichl, central Carinthia. This has been dated to at least 320 BC–over 1,600 years earlier than the oldest Scottish tartan, which dates from 1300 AD. Many Austrian stores now sell Austrian kilts alongside lederhosen.

THE WORLD'S LARGEST AND MOST VALUABLE LUMPS

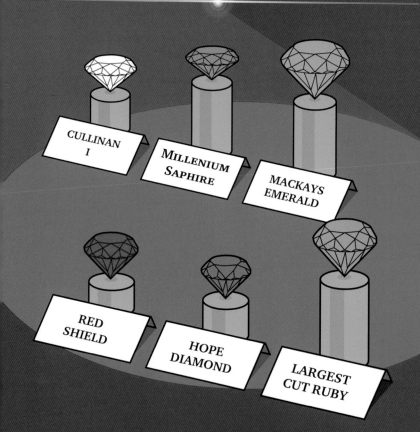

CULLINAN I

MILLENIUM SAPHIRE

MACKAYS EMERALD

RED SHIELD

HOPE DIAMOND

LARGEST CUT RUBY

Most objects in our world are measured within standard weight and measurement systems, but people within the precious material world use their own system entirely: they can be said to 'measure in beans'. The word 'carat' is thought to have come from the carob bean, whose consistent weight was used in days gone by to measure gem stones. Nowadays, carats are used slightly differently to measure both gem stones and gold.

For gem stones and pearls:
1 carat = 200 milligrams/0.2 grams/ 0.007 ounces

You could put it another way: imagine one kilo of proper carrots. A one kilo bag of carrots is equal to 5,000 one carat diamonds.

Gold	
24 carat	pure gold
22 carat	91.67 per cent gold
18 carat	75 per cent gold

The value out of 24 is used to describe the purity of the gold.

What is the biggest piece of gold ever found? Well, there is a huge piece of gold called the "Hand of Faith" which weighs in at 62 pounds, or 28.12 kilos. It is the largest piece of naturally occurring gold known to be in existence and was found in Australia with a metal detector in 1980. Imagine the excitement when the buzzing started on the metal detector and this enormous lump of gold was dug out of the ground! It was bought for a million dollars by The Golden Nugget Casino, and there it proudly stands to this day in a glass case. If you look at a picture of it, you can see why it is called the Hand of Faith because it does indeed look like a hand, albeit with a couple of fingers missing.

What about gem stones? The largest sapphire is called 'The Millennium Sapphire' and it was found in Madagascar in 1995. It is 61,500 carats and weighs nearly 18 kilos with an estimated value of up to 500 million dollars. The largest cut sapphire is the 'Blue Giant of the Orient' at 466 carats.

If you have quite a few spare million dollars floating around you could buy the world's largest cut ruby, which weighs 3.7 kilos, is 18,696 carats, and measures roughly 12 x 11 x 13 centimetres. The largest uncut ruby however is more than twice that, at 8.18 kilos.

Many people's favourite gem stones are emeralds. The largest known uncut emerald is called "The Gachala Emerald" and it weighs in at 858 carats. It sits in the Smithsonian Museum in the United States and was donated by the New York jeweller Harry Winston. The "Mackay Emerald" in the National Gem Collection—the largest cut emerald—has been set into a Cartier-designed necklace and is 167.97 carats (33 grams in weight). The largest emerald in the world though, is the Moghul emerald at 217.8 carats.

Continued…

When it comes to diamonds, size is not everything. Shape and cut are extremely important, but the most valuable quality in diamonds is their hue, with red being by far the rarest and worth the most. The Moussaieff

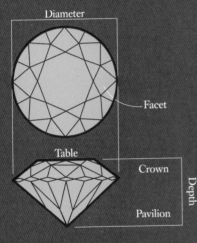

Diameter

Facet

Table

Crown

Pavilion

Depth

Red diamond or Red Shield is believed by some to be the single most expensive item on earth, even though at just under six carats, it is relatively small. Going on size however, the largest known cut diamond is reckoned to be the Cullinan I or the Star of Africa. This pear-shaped monster weighs in at 530.20 carats, measures about six by 4.5 by 2.8 centimetres, and is presently the centrepiece of the King Edward VII sceptre, owned by the British Royal Family. It is not for

sale, so it is difficult to put a value on it, but is estimated to be worth in the region of £200 million, or just over $322 million.

Then there is the Hope Diamond, which is a very rare blue. It is 45.52 carats and was once owned, in the 1700s, by King Louis XIV of France. It then did the rounds, being owned by various extremely rich families and was eventually donated to the Smithsonian Institute in Washington, DC. Although much smaller than the Star of Africa, the Hope Diamond is estimated to be worth between £150 to £175 million–that is about $250 million–because of its very rare blue colour.

Yet these are just grains of sand compared to the largest diamond in the whole universe. It exists 50 light years away, in the Centaurus constellation, within the compressed heart of an old burnt-out star, now known as a white dwarf, which was once very much like our own sun. It is, in fact, an enormously huge diamond that is 4,000 kilometres or 2,485.5 miles across and far too big to wear around anyone's neck. In carat terms it is estimated to be 10 billion, trillion, trillion carats. Astronomers apparently call it "Lucy", after The Beatles' song *Lucy in the Sky with Diamonds*. They say that when our own sun dies in five billion years, it too will become a white dwarf, and its ember core will crystallise, leaving a giant diamond in the centre of our solar system.

RATS

POPULATING THE WORLD

Rats populate just about every place that we humans do, apart from Antarctica and the Arctic. It has been said that rats are the second most successful species on the planet after humans. The brown rat is by far the most common, and he is the one that most of us will have caught sight of at some point. He is also sometimes referred to as the Norwegian Rat, but most experts think this is rather a misleading term, with many favouring Asia as their probable place of origin. Rats will hitch a ride on just about anything they can climb onto, and as ships started travelling further and further afield, so did the rats.

Stories about rats have been vastly exaggerated over the years, and many urban myths abound, such as, "You are never more than ten feet away from a rat", or, "there are some rats around that are as big as cats". The fact is that a brown rat can grow to a maximum length of around nine or ten inches, but then the tail can be another nine or ten inches, in effect doubling its length.

Rats are usually most active during the night whilst us humans are asleep. They are also very good swimmers, and have been known to come up from sewers into toilet bowls and bite people from underneath. Apparently, rats have a very good sense of humour; some experts believe that the chirping noise made by rats is the equivalent of our human laugh.

Rats tend to stay in gangs, and although they can live for up to about three years, they are more likely to die prematurely after only one year. There are many reasons for this, including humans poisoning them, and many are killed by each other. A female brown rat can have four or five litters a year, each producing five to 10 babies. They tend to live around humans because they can scavenge on left-over food, but where no humans are present, they prefer a damp environment such as a river bank. New York is supposed to be the rat capital of the world, with some estimates claiming a rat population of up to 100 million.

Rats have been known to attack and kill chickens, birds and ducks. Very rarely, they have also been known to attack homeless people sleeping rough.

Despite all of the above, there are people who love to keep rats as pets. There is an organisation in the UK called The National Fancy Rat Society, and they do all kinds of activities, such as hosting shows around the UK, and offering advice on keeping rats.

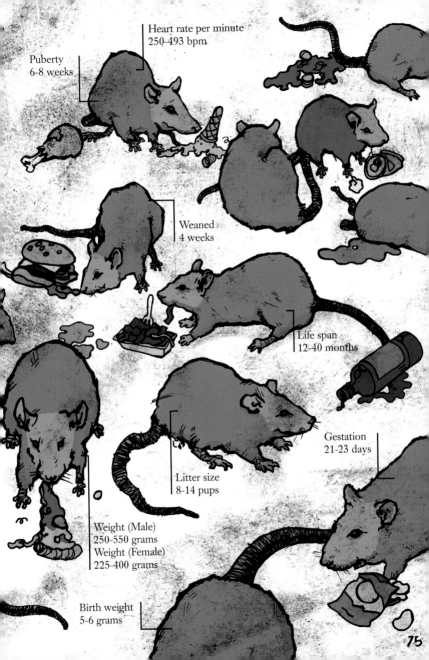

Heart rate per minute
250-493 bpm

Puberty
6-8 weeks

Weaned
4 weeks

Life span
12-40 months

Gestation
21-23 days

Litter size
8-14 pups

Weight (Male)
250-550 grams
Weight (Female)
225-400 grams

Birth weight
5-6 grams

75

WHO DECIDES WHEN EASTER IS?

The early church celebrated Easter on different days of the week until 325 AD, when the rule that: "Easter shall be celebrated on the first Sunday after the full moon, on or after, the vernal equinox" was adopted by the Council of Nicaea—a Roman council of Christian bishops. This means that the actual date for Easter can be as early as the 22 March or as late as 25 April.

Until 325 AD, Easter was celebrated as a moveable feast on a Friday, Saturday or Sunday in March. The Emperor Constantine decided to try and fix a definitive date, but unfortunately left it in the hands of the bureaucrats, with the Council of Nicaea devising a more complicated system. Their Easter Rule said that the festival should be celebrated on the first Sunday that occurs after the full moon, on or after, what is known as the vernal equinox—20 March—or the first official day of Spring. To make the date even harder to work out, the ecclesiastical full moon often falls on a different day from the astronomical full moon. But Easter will always be between the dates of 22 March and 25 April.

In basic terms; "Easter falls on the first Sunday that comes after the first full moon that falls after the first day of Spring."

Milk

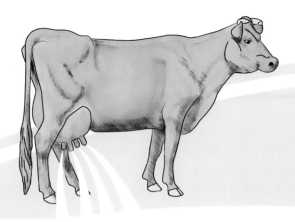

Milk is the primary source of nutrition for young mammals until they are able to take in other forms of food. In early infancy, a mother's milk is not only a source of food but also contains antibodies, which reduce the risk of infection and disease to the baby.

But, did you know that humans are the only species that consciously drink milk after infancy, and the milk of another species at that? Milk contains vitamins A and B, calcium, zinc and magnesium; it also strengthens bones and teeth, is excellent for rehydration, and its fatty acids are said to be very good for the skin.

Humans have been consuming milk beyond infancy for thousands of years; however, we have not always been able to digest it. Our bodies have had to evolve in order to be able to digest a component of milk called lactose, which is a form of natural sugar. There are still many people throughout the world who cannot digest milk properly because they are lactose intolerant, which gives them digestion problems. There are others who link drinking milk and milk products to arthritis, respiratory problems and allergies.

The milk glands in cows, as in other mammals, are in fact very large and modified sweat glands. With intensive milk production comes the high risk of infection; according to the Vegetarian and Vegan Foundation, every litre of milk is legally allowed to contain up to 400 million pus cells. In order to keep up with high milk production demands, a cow must continuously breed and produce calves.

Although many of us automatically think of 'milk' as meaning cow's milk, the milk of sheep, goats, camels, water buffalo, yaks and horses is also widely consumed throughout the world. For some top chefs, horse milk has become a prized culinary ingredient.

OUR MASSIVE SOLAR SYSTEM

The enormity of our solar system is rarely explained in such a way that makes sense; but the distances between the planets and their sizes in relation to the sun are really worth getting your head around.

Here is a walking trip you can use to visualise the size of the sun, the planets and just how far away they are from each other, in 11 easy steps:

1. First, imagine placing an enormous beachball, three metres in diameter, outside your front door. This beachball is the sun.

2. Then choose the direction from your front door that is the most familiar to you, and walk about 125 metres.

3. At 125 metres, you will find the planet closest to the sun: Mercury. Mercury would be just one centimetre in diameter—approximately the size of a kidney bean.

4. From Mercury, carry on walking a further 108 metres until you are nearly a quarter of a mile from your front door, and here you will find Venus, which would be 2.6 centimetres in diameter; the size of a strawberry.

5. Walk on for a further 89 metres, and you come to planet Earth, which would be 2.7 centimetres in size; marginally bigger than the last strawberry. In real terms, you would now be 93 million miles from the sun. That's about 3,720 times the Earth's circumference.

10

9

11

6. Now walk a further 169 metres to Mars; at 1.4 centimetres, that will be about the size of a marble.

7. Next, you would have to walk a little over a mile—another 1,186 metres— before you came to the giant planet Jupiter. Jupiter comes in at roughly the size of a watermelon or 30 centimetres in diameter.

8. Another mile and a half, and you will find Saturn, about 25 centimetres in diameter: a bit bigger than a soccer ball.

9. The next walk is very nearly two miles, where you will find Uranus, which we could compare to a softball

10. Off we go hiking again for just over two miles before we come across Neptune, which is a ball just a tiny bit smaller than Uranus.

11. Another 1.8 miles along the road, and you'll come across a very small five millimetre pea, which is the smallest, coldest planet, and also the furthest away from the Sun: Pluto.

Altogether you would have walked very nearly eight miles from your front door, where the beachball of a sun is still. If you were to walk on to the nearest star to our solar system, Alpha Centauri, that would be a further 54,000 miles—which is twice the distance

GREAT PYRAMID OF KHUFU *

LOCATION	Giza, Egypt
DATE	2560 BC
HEIGHT	137 m
VOLUME	2.58 million m³

SPECIAL FEATURES
Apex corresponds to the North Pole
Perimeter of its base correlates to the
circumference of the equator.

PYRAMID OF KHAFRE

LOCATION	Giza, Egypt
DATE	2558 BC
HEIGHT	131.5 m
VOLUME	2.21 million m³

SPECIAL FEATURES
Topmost layer of smooth stones are the only
remaining casing stones on a Giza Pyramid

GREAT PYRAMID OF CHOLULA * *

LOCATION	Puebla, Mexico
DATE	2 BC
HEIGHT	55 m
VOLUME	4.45 million m³

SPECIAL FEATURES
Catholic church on top of it
Built for Queztlcoatl, the Feathered Serpent
God

LUXOR PYRAMID

LOCATION	Las Vegas, USA
DATE	1993
HEIGHT	110 m
VOLUME	1.2 million m³

SPECIAL FEATURES
2,526 guest rooms
Gigantic casino area, showroom, restaurants,
and entertainment venues on 2nd floor

0.9–2.8 million

SPECIAL FEATURES
If you broke the Great pyram
30 cm thick you could build
high that would stretch all
around France!

82

WHO HAS THE BEST PYRAMID?

The ancient Egyptian pyramids have enthralled people right through the ages, and for many years, great numbers of mathematicians and scientists have been falling over each other to understand how and why they were built. Ambitious rulers such as Napoleon and the Roman emperors were fascinated by ancient Egyptian power structures and intrigued by the associated mysteries of the Pyramids, believing that some key to power could be found there.

When Sir Isaac Newton came to measure the Great Pyramid of Khufu at Giza–the oldest built structure in existence–with a view to determining the earth's size from its dimensions, he got more than he bargained for. He initially measured in conventional inches, and found very little, but when he then converted these dimensions into ancient Jewish inches, he was astonished to find measurements which equate exactly to the days of the year–even including leap years–along with other unbelievable statistical coincidences, such as:

- One face of the pyramid represents one curved quadrant of the Northern Hemisphere.
- Twice the height of the pyramid, divided by the circumference of its base, equals Pi.

- The apex of The Great Pyramid corresponds to the North Pole, while the perimeter of its base correlates to the circumference of the equator.
- If you draw intersecting lines on a globe, north–south and east–west, making them pass directly through the middle of the greatest amount of land mass, these lines will intersect on the exact spot where the Great Pyramid stands. There are only two places on earth where these two lines can cross, and the other one is in the middle of the Pacific Ocean.

Now, how did the ancient Egyptians manage to do that when so little was known at that time about the rest of the world? Are these findings all just a huge coincidence? Such mysteries still remain unanswered. And spooky correlations aside, how did they manage to build this Great Pyramid in the first place? It is made up of approximately 2.3 million blocks of limestone, ranging in weight from 2.26 tonnes, and up to 63.5 tonnes–that is the weight of about 70 family cars for one single block. Many claim that the Great Pyramid could not even be built to the same exacting standards today with all our technology and equipment,

Continued...

so how did they do it four and a half thousand years ago? Some even insist that it and the other pyramids at Giza could only have been built under the instruction of highly intelligent extra-terrestrial beings!

The Great Pyramid of Khufu is certainly the highest ancient pyramid in the world, at 137 metres tall, and 2.58 million metres^3 in volume. But Egypt is not the only place in the world with impressive and mysterious pyramids. In fact, if you are talking about size in terms of volume, rather than height, the Great Pyramid of Cholula in Mexico can be said to be the biggest pyramid in the world, at 4.45 million metres^3. At first glance, it looks like a hill with a Catholic church on top, but underneath there is an enormous pyramid, which used to be a temple to the Feathered Serpent God, Quetzalcoatl, built in stages between the third century BC and the ninth century AD.

There are really impressive correlations between the positions of the Mexican pyramids and their exact alignment with the stars and solar system. The six hundred pyramids at the ancient city of Teotihuacan, built by the Mayan people, line up precisely with certain stars and planets. These people had a very advanced understanding of astronomy, mathematics, and geometry, over and beyond what the rest of the world knew at that time. The whole city of Teotihuacan is dominated by the Pyramid of the Sun, which is 1.2 million metres^3 and 75 metres high. It is built directly over a natural cave, rediscovered as recently as 1971, which the local population believed was a gateway to the next world. Just like the Great Pyramid in Egypt, the ratio of the height of the Pyramid of the Sun to the perimeter of its base comes from the mathematical rule of Pi. It originally had a wooden temple on the top, from which there would have been spectacular views over the city of Teotihuacan below.

One of the most fascinating discoveries made at the Mayan pyramids is the presence of a very fragile material called mica, which is a kind of mineral with unique properties, commonly used nowadays for laser devices, medical electronics and radar systems. The nearest place to the Mayan pyramids where mica is found is 2,000 miles away in Brazil; yet huge quantities were somehow transported over that vast distance to use as an inner layer on Mexican pyramids. How they did it is a massive question in itself; but why did they bring it? It was used as an inner layer of the pyramid, and therefore could not be seen from the outside, so what was its purpose? This mystery remains unsolved.

One of the most exciting recent pyramid discoveries is in Japan. In 1996, a building structure resembling the remains of a stepped pyramid was discovered by a sports diver under only 75 feet of water, and caused great excitement amongst archeologists. It has been dated at around 8000 BC, which makes it almost twice as old as the Great Pyramid. It would have stood at around 90 feet high and 600 feet wide, and it even has what looks like a road running round it. It is generally accepted that the unknown civilisation that built it 10,000 years ago must have had a very high level of technology, and that there must have been some kind of machinery involved.

So, who has the best pyramid?

BENT PYRAMID

Bent

2600BC

PYRAMID OF THE SUN

LOCATION Teotihuacán, Valley of Mexico

DATE 2 AD

HEIGHT 75 m

VOLUME 1.2 million m³

SPECIAL FEATURES
Internal layer of mica, transported from 2,000 miles away
Connected to Moon Pyramid
the Dead

TRANSAMERICA PYRAMID

LOCATION San Francisco, USA

DATE 1972

HEIGHT 260 m

VOLUME 252,720 m³

SPECIAL FEATURES
Designed as the ideal shape for city-centre skyscrapers, letting more air and light in the adjacent streets
It takes two months to clean its 3,678 windows

US

1993

Washing

THE LOUVRE

LOCATION Paris, France

DATE 1989

HEIGHT 20.6 m

VOLUME 8411.67 m³

SPECIAL FEATURES
Constructed with an entrance lobby underneath to relieve the Louvre's historical entrance of 30,000 daily visitors
Rumoured to be made up of 666 glass rhomboids.

FEATURES
inclination, but the top section
he shallower angle of 43 degre

FEATURES

Las Vegas,

19

PE

260

85

9-2.8 million m³
the tallest man-made stru

THE ROSETTA STONE

The richness of ancient Egyptian civilisation, which ran for over three thousand years from 3500 to 322 BC, has intrigued scholars, scientists and archeologists for centuries. Yet the writing system of the ancient Egyptians–hieroglyphics–remained a mystery until the French campaign in Egypt under Napoleon I in 1799, when the French were carrying out construction work in the port of Rosetta. There they discovered an upright stone–now referred to as the Rosetta Stone–that measured around 114 x 71 x 28 centimetres and weighed 762 kilos or 1680 pounds. The Stone featured an inscribed surface–stele–with inscriptions written in three different languages: hieroglyphics, Demotic and classical Greek, all of which helped to first translate hieroglyphics.

The University of Pennsylvania published the first complete translation of the Stone, 59 years after its initial discovery. Here it emerged that the meaning of the text itself was relatively banal–it is basically a tax exemption document for priests. However, without this discovery, it is possible that scholars would still be scratching their heads.

What happened to the Rosetta Stone? Well, in 1801, two years after the French invasion of Egypt, the British followed suit with the capture of the capital Alexandria, and a huge row erupted as to who owned artefacts that the French had originally found. Rumour has it that the Stone was taken to Britain by Colonel Tomkyns Hilgrove Turner, strapped to a gun carriage on a captured French ship, and that the French had to make do with a plaster cast of the Stone. It now stands in The British Museum.

Guano

Throughout its history, Peru has been famed for three main exports: gold, silver, and guano. What is guano? Well, it is the excrement of birds, in this case, and it can also be the excrement of other animals, such as bats and seals. Peru once built up an absolute fortune by exporting guano, and amongst the biggest importers were the British.

Peruvian guano comes mainly from the Guanay Cormorant and the Peruvian Booby bird; the Incas are known to have used guano as a fertilizer in the fifteenth and sixteenth centuries. Around the mid-nineteenth century, farmers around the developed world started to appreciate the benefits of guano as a fertiliser due to its high content of phosphorus and nitrogen. This triggered a 'guano rush', and in just one year—1858—the UK imported just short of 300,000 tonnes of Peruvian guano to be used as farm fertiliser. The British had a virtual world monopoly of guano, which alarmed the US so much that the then President, Millard Fillmore, made an address to the State of the Union: "Peruvian guano has become so desirable that it is the duty of the Government to employ all the means properly in its power for the purpose of causing that article to be imported into the country at a reasonable price."

Guano must have been almost as desirable as oil is today. A 'Guano Islands Act' was even created, the first clause of which is:

"Whenever any citizen of the United States discovers a deposit of guano on any island, rock, or key, not within the lawful jurisdiction of any other government, and not occupied by the citizens of any other government, and takes peaceable possession thereof, and occupies the same, such island, rock, or key may, at the discretion of the President, be considered as appertaining to the United States."

Following this act, about 60 islands in the Caribbean and Pacific were acquired by the Americans for their guano resources.

Peru must have been like the Saudi Arabia of guano, because during its 40 year hey-day of 1840–1880, Peru was able to pay off all of its foreign debt with the proceeds. Peru exported over 18 million tonnes of guano in just 40 years. Unfortunately for them, there were also a few entrepreneurial people around in Britain during the Industrial Revolution who started manufacturing a commercial equivalent, which overtook Peruvian guano in sales and pushed it out of the British market.

What happened to all the Lard?

THEY'RE HAPPY
Because they eat
LARD

Issued by the Lard Information Council

For many years, lard was a common ingredient in lots of domestic kitchens; people can remember their grandmothers only ever using lard in pastry, or keeping a whole lot of lard permanently sitting—or so it seemed—in their fryers; it was even quite normal to spread lard on your bread and make a sandwich of it.

Lard is made from pork fat, which is either heated on its own—'dry rendered'—or in water, with the fat that rises to the top skimmed off and set aside, called "wet rendering". It is relatively easy to make at home from offcuts, and doing so used to be pretty commonplace.

Nowadays though, lard is generally seen as being unhealthy. Most people use some kind of oil for frying, such as sunflower oil, vegetable oil or olive oil. As for pastry, vegetable shortening—which is solid vegetable fat—or butter is generally used. And spreading your morning toast with lard is almost unheard of; butter or margarine is far more common. So what happened to all the lard we used to consume—are we missing a trick here?

As is turns out, we might be. If you look at the make-up of lard, butter and vegetable fat products, you find that there are four main kinds of fats, some of which are better for you than others.

Trans fats are produced artificially in a process called hydrogenation, which turns liquid vegetable oil into solid fat; this gives products like biscuits and cakes a longer shelf life. Trans fats can raise cholesterol. Too much cholesterol will clog your arteries, which can eventually lead to a heart attack. Trans fats have also been linked to Alzheimer's disease and certain cancers.

Saturated fats occur naturally in animal fats such as butter, cheese, cream, meat, and lard. There are different kinds of saturated fats; but consuming too much can also directly raise cholesterol levels—see above.

Continued...

They're young... They're in love...
They eat LARD

©1957. Issued by The British Lard Marketing Board in conjunction with the Department of Health.

British Lard
Marketing Board

Monounsaturated fats are found along with saturated fat in the above animal fats; and also in olives and avocados. Monounsaturated fats can actually reduce cholesterol levels in your blood, and lower your risk of heart disease and stroke. They are also high in the antioxidant vitamin E.

Polyunsaturated fats can also reduce cholesterol, so like monounsaturated fats, they are better for you. They are found in vegetable oils, including soybean oil, corn oil and safflower oil, nuts and seeds, and fatty fish such as salmon, mackerel, herring and trout.

When you compare lard to butter, lard has only around three quarters of the cholesterol-raising saturated fat of butter. Lard also has more than double the monounsaturated fat of butter, and almost four times the

polyunsaturated fat—both of which lower cholesterol. In comparison to margarine and vegetable oils, lard contains absolutely no trans fats. And, like duck and goose fat, even the saturated fat in lard is said to have a neutral effect on blood cholesterol. Many top chefs swear by lard for certain recipes, especially flaky, moist pie crusts and croissants, and wet-rendered lard certainly has a higher smoking point than other fats, which means that foods fried in it absorb less grease.

You only have to say the word "Lard" and many people will screw their faces up—maybe because of its association as a 'poor' food, maybe because of the marketing of margarine and dairy fats—but it appears that lard may have been unfairly given a bad name.

Seven Easy Steps to Rendering Your Own Lard

Ingredients:
Pig fat
Water 1/2 cup
Sterilised Jars

1. Ask your local butcher for a pound of pig fat. "Leaf lard" from around the pig's kidneys is the best kind of fat for baking. "Fat back" is better for frying. Chop your fat up into little cubes.

2. Heat the chopped fat with about half a cup of water in a large, heavy pot on a low heat, stirring every ten minutes.

3. When after about an hour the fat starts melting and making loud popping noises—this noise is the air escaping and little pieces of fried pork or 'cracklings' forming—start stirring more often. The cracklings will rise to the surface.

4. Keep up the frequent stirring; take care the popping fat does not burn you. After a while, the cracklings will sink to the bottom.

5. The lard is now rendered. Let it cool.

6. Strain the cooled lard through a colander or cotton strainer into sterilised jars. The cracklings will be caught in the strainer; these can be eaten as a snack.

7. Put the jars of yellowish liquid into the refrigerator overnight; next morning it will be white and more solid.

You can now use your home-rendered lard for your baking and frying needs, or spread on toast as 'dripping'. It will keep in the refrigerator for three months.

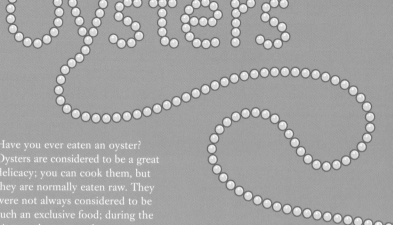

Oysters

Have you ever eaten an oyster? Oysters are considered to be a great delicacy; you can cook them, but they are normally eaten raw. They were not always considered to be such an exclusive food; during the nineteenth century, they were an abundant source of food for the poor in coastal Britain, France and the United States. But as their popularity grew, oyster beds decreased, so foreign varieties were then introduced. Unfortunately, with the foreign varieties came disease, and this combined with increased pollution reduced stocks massively, making them the rare commodity they are today, enjoyed only by those who can afford them.

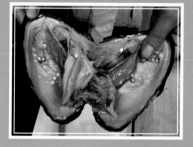

At first glance, you cannot tell whether an oyster is male or female–in actual fact they change their sex one or more times during their lives. They usually spend their first year as a male, and then become female, laying up to 100 million eggs a year. These eggs are sprayed into the water, and they hatch about ten hours later–each one the size of a pinprick. Within 24 hours, they begin to grow their shell, and stick themselves onto a rock on the sea-bed.

The average lifespan of an oyster is about six years, but they have been known to live for up to 20 years, and can grow as long as 30 centimetres–which is about a foot in length. Can you imagine opening a foot-long oyster and pouring it down your throat?

Although oysters are expensive, they're actually a poor energy source, with a dozen live oysters only containing around 110 calories. Also, a word of

warning, fresh oysters—that is, uncooked oysters—must always be eaten alive, because if you eat one that is already dead you can be poisoned. Live oysters usually have a closed shell, but that is not always the case. If you are given an oyster with an open shell, you have to tap the shell, and if the oyster is still alive the shell will close up immediately, indicating that it is fit for purpose.

Pearl oysters are not closely related to the edible oysters, so there are no fortunes waiting to be found overnight in a pile of oysters. Pearl oysters are of a completely different family called "feathered oysters", or *pteriidae*. Both natural and cultured pearls come from this species. Most people know that not every one of these kinds of oyster produces a pearl, but it is quite surprising to learn that a three-tonne haul of pearl-bearing oysters would only yield about four pearls. That is why they are so very

expensive; a very high quality natural pearl necklace can now fetch a few hundred thousand pounds.

Cleverly, the oysters produce the pearls in order to overcome the presence of a parasite. If a parasite gets into the oyster's shell, it is soon coated in a composite produced by the oyster, which is called nacre. Over a number of years, this parasite is then covered with layer upon layer of nacre creating a natural pearl. So, a pearl is really a very high-class coffin for a parasite. At the beginning of the twentieth century, researchers realised that they could trick oysters into producing pearls by placing a tiny piece of polished mussel shell inside the oyster, who mistakes it for a parasite. The oyster then proceeds to coat it with nacre, thereby creating a cultured pearl.

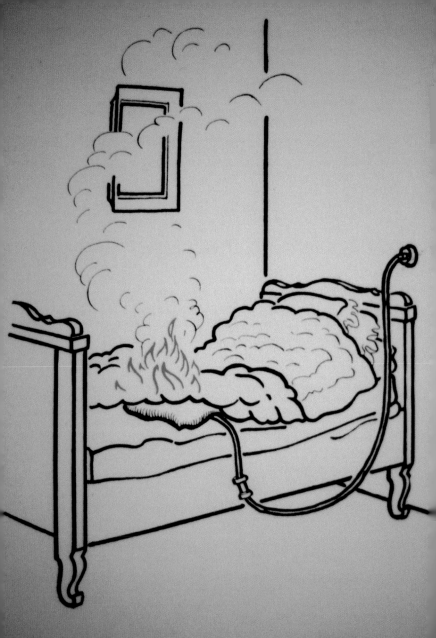

If ever you look closely at the flames of an open fire, you will realise that it is a very strange phenomenon. We all know that fire consists of flames, and that it is hot, but what exactly is it and how does it come about?

The Encyclopedia Britannica calls it: "The rapid burning of combustible material with the evolution of heat and usually accompanied by flame." But does a proper fire not always have flames?

Another definition is as follows: "Typically, fire comes from a chemical reaction between oxygen in the atmosphere and some sort of fuel i.e. wood, petrol etc.." But what are the flames?

We are told that "oxygen, fuel and heat are the ingredients of a fire". That tells us what we need for fire to happen; but what about what fire actually is?

This is the chemical equation:

$$CH_2O + O_2 \rightarrow H_2O + CO_2 + CO + C + N_2$$

The full answer that we are looking for is this: flames are actually glowing gas. As a fuel heats up, it releases gases which ignite when mixed within oxygen. Different colours are caused by varying temperatures within the flames. Flames cool as they rise, so the hottest part of the flame is blue at the bottom, changing colour to orange in the middle and then yellow at the top.

Birds on a Wire

Why do birds face the same way whilst sat on a power line? The answer is that they always face into the wind. There are three main reasons for this:

1. Birds have to take off against the wind; if they took off with the wind behind them, it would ruffle their feathers and knock them off-balance. So when they come into land and sit on power lines, they have to be facing into the wind; this is how they stay sitting, until they take off again.

2. They need to retain body heat, because facing the wind presses their feathers to their body and keeps the heat in.

3. Taking off into the wind gives them lift, just as an aeroplane takes off into the wind on the same principle.

If you watch a flock of birds sat on a telegraph or power line on a very calm day, you may see some of them facing in one direction and others facing in the opposite direction. This

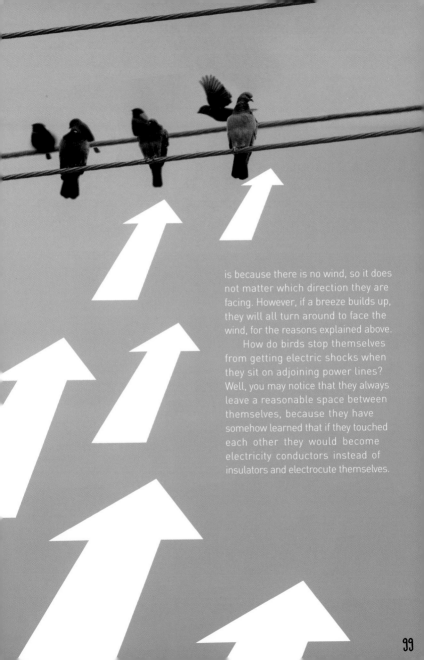

is because there is no wind, so it does not matter which direction they are facing. However, if a breeze builds up, they will all turn around to face the wind, for the reasons explained above.

How do birds stop themselves from getting electric shocks when they sit on adjoining power lines? Well, you may notice that they always leave a reasonable space between themselves, because they have somehow learned that if they touched each other they would become electricity conductors instead of insulators and electrocute themselves.

Colossus of Rhodes

Temple of Artemis

Hanging Gardens of Babylon

Statue of Zeus at Olympia

Great pyramid of Giza

Lighthouse of Alexandria

Mausoleum of Maussollus

The Seven Wonders of the World

If someone were to ask you, "What are the original Seven Wonders of the World?" would you be able to answer them correctly? Most people could perhaps get a couple, or at least one of them. How many do you know? The full list is below. How many of them still exist? In actual fact, only one of them has not been destroyed by wars and earthquakes–and that is the Great Pyramid at Giza, Egypt.

Who decided on them in the first place? There does not appear to be a definitive answer, but there are a few suggestions:

- The Greek historian Herodutus
- The Greek writer Antipater
- The Greek scholar Callimachus of Cyrene at the Museum of Alexandria
- The Byzantine mathematician and traveller Philon.

Great pyramid at Giza, Egypt

Hanging Gardens of Babylon, Iraq

Statue of Zeus at Olympia, Greece

Temple of Artemis at Ephesus, Turkey

Mausoleum of Maussollus at Halicarnassus, Turkey

Lighthouse of Alexandria, Egypt

Colossus of Rhodes, Greece

Continued...

The Greeks had a huge and very influential empire that spanned what we now call Egypt and Turkey, the Middle East, and almost as far as India, so it is perhaps not surprising that all Seven of these Wonders should fall within the Greek Empire.

As the time when the Seven Wonders were decided–sometime between 484 and 130 BC–was such a long time ago, and six out of the seven are no longer in existence, there is now an organisation called The New7Wonders Foundation, who organised a poll to decide a new list of The Seven Wonders of the World. This poll attracted almost one hundred million votes worldwide and the results were announced in Lisbon, Portugal, in 2007.

Here are the new Seven Wonders:

The Coliseum, Rome

The Taj Mahal, India

The Great Wall of China

The Ancient City of Petra, Jordan

The Inca Ruins at Machu Picchu, Peru

The Ancient City of Chichén Itzá, Mexico

The Christ Redeemer Statue in Rio de Janeiro, Brazil

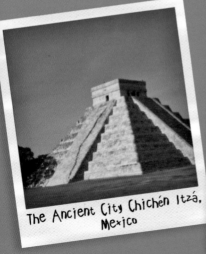

The Ancient City Chichén Itzá, Mexico

The Great Wall of China

The Christ Redeemer Statue, Brazil

The Ancient City of Petra, Jordan

The Inca Ruins at Machu Picchu, Peru

The Coliseum, Rome

The Taj Mahal, India

103

MH Electrons ARE COMING !

THUNDER AND LIGHTNING

When people experience a thunderstorm, more often than not they will say, "it's thundering and lightning". This seems odd, because lightning appears to come before thunder. On that basis, should we really be saying, "it's lightning and thundering"? Well no, because thunder and lightning actually occur at virtually the same time. The reason lightning seems to come before thunder is because the speed of light is much faster than the speed of sound, so the light reaches you before the sound does.

When for example a strike happens three kilometres away, the light from the lightning will reach you in around ten milliseconds. The sound wave–thunder–arrives more slowly, in around ten seconds. Because sound lessens with distance, thunder can seldom be heard from more than ten miles away; but storms can move very quickly, and if you see lightning and then hear thunder within 30 seconds or less, then there is a chance that the next strike may be roughly where you are standing.

But what exactly is thunder and lightning? Well, lightning is basically an electrical current. Frozen raindrops bump into each other as they move around within a cloud, creating an electrical charge. These build up until the cloud is full of

Continued...

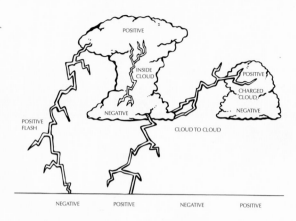

these electrical charges. A positive charge builds up at the top of the cloud and a negative charge builds up at the bottom of the cloud. Because opposites attract, this causes the positive charge to build up on the ground beneath the cloud. A charge from a cloud will eventually make a connection with a charge within a building or a tree, and–'pow!'–lightning happens.

As for the thunder, that is from an immediate increase in pressure and temperature from the lightning, which makes the surrounding air expand violently, faster than the speed of sound, with a 'bang' of thunder. It is a bit like the sonic boom associated with a jet fighter plane.

Bolts of lightning only have a diameter of 2.5 to five centimetres, so it is quite frightening to learn that they can heat the air around them up to about 30,000 °C in a matter of milliseconds. In terms of the proportion of sound to light and heat within the electrical energy of lightning, less than one per cent of it is converted into sound or thunder, around ten per cent is light and the remainder is heat.

The smelliest plant in the world

select variety

strong top for heavy scent

Native to the tropical forests of Sumatra in Indonesia is a flowering plant known as the *Titan Arum*. This plant stinks so bad that it is commonly referred to as the "corpse flower".

Its Latin name is *Amorphophallus titanium*, which roughly translates as "enormous shapeless phallus"–and it is reported to be the world's biggest flower at around nine feet high and four feet wide. That is when it flowers at all, which is a very rare occurrence, happening only every few years.

When it does bloom, the flower only lasts for about a day, so you would be very lucky indeed to see it; on the other hand, you may be more lucky not to see it bloom because that is when this disgusting smell comes off it, rather like the stench of rotting flesh. People have often been known to gag, vomit, and even faint in its company, and it is said that the odour can be detected from half a mile away.

There is, of course, a perfectly good reason why *Titan Arum* stinks like it does, and that is to attract the carrion beetles and flies that help it to pollinate. London's Kew Gardens own a *Titum Arum*, as does the University of California, Davis–who has named theirs "Ted". There is one called "Mr Stinky" at Fairfield Tropical Gardens in Coral Gables, Florida, and one called "Tiny" who lives at University College Santa Barbara.

On the last occasion that Tiny sprang to life, the aroma was described as being "like rotten eggs laid by a decaying chicken in a clogged drainpipe".

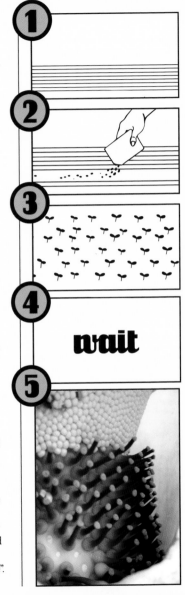

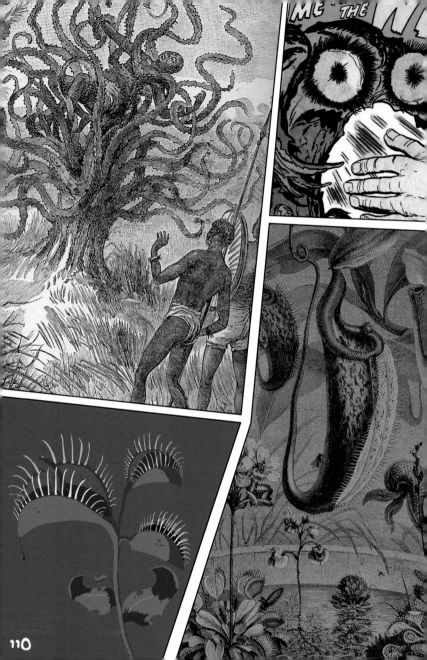

CARNIVOROUS PLANTS

There are a lot of myths about carnivorous plants. In reality, carnivorous plants eat flies and arthropods such as spiders, beetles and butterflies, and they use a trapping mechanism to catch and then consume their prey.

The reason these plants are carnivorous is because the soil where they grow—usually bogs and rocky outcroppings—does not give them enough nutrients, so they have developed a taste for insects.

One of the most common carnivorous plants that we see in peoples' houses is the fly-eating Venus Flytrap. Because they eat things, some people who keep these plants think of them as pets rather than plants and give them names, rather like those people who look after incredibly smelly plants.

Venus Flytraps can easily be bought, but if you do so, be careful not to prod the trap in order to see it close. This uses up a lot of energy for the plant, especially when there are no nutrients involved. Not surprisingly, this is one of the main reasons behind high incidences of Flytraps dying soon after purchase. Another very common reason is people feeding them with food that is not insects, such as bits of hamburger or cheese.

CONTINUED...

BEWARE THE TRIFFIDS... they grow ...know...walk...talk...stalk...and KILL!

From the greatest science-fiction novel of all time!

THE DAY OF THE TRIFFIDS

IN **CinemaSCOPE** AND **EASTMANCOLOR**

STARRING

HOWARD KEEL
NICOLE MAUREY

Executive Producer
PHILIP YORDAN · GEORGE PITCHER · STEVE SEKELY · PHILIP YORDAN
Produced by   Directed by   Screenplay by

From the Novel by JOHN WYNDHAM
Author of "VILLAGE OF THE DAMNED"

A SECURITY PICTURES LTD. PRODUCTION
AN ALLIED ARTISTS RELEASE

112

THE FIVE CATEGORIES OF CARNIVOROUS PLANT:

PITFALL TRAPS

THESE PLANTS USE A ROLLED-UP LEAF CONTAINING DIGESTIVE ENZYMES AND BACTERIA TO TRAP THEIR PREY.

FLYPAPER TRAPS

A GLUE-LIKE MUCUS SUBSTANCE MEANS THAT INSECTS LANDING ON THE PLANT GET STUCK AND THEN EATEN.

BLADDER TRAPS

THESE HAVE HANGING 'BLADDERS', AND ANY INSECT ALIGHTING ON IT TRIGGERS A VACUUM OF TINY HAIRS WITHIN THE BLADDER. THE PREY IS THEN SUCKED INSIDE AND DIGESTED.

LOBSTER-POT TRAPS

THESE PLANTS HAVE A BRISTLE-LINED CHAMBER WHICH IS EASY FOR INSECTS TO ENTER, BUT CANNOT BE EXITED BECAUSE THE BRISTLES ALL POINT INWARD.

SNAP!

SNAP TRAPS

THESE 'JAWS' CLOSE RAPIDLY ONCE TRIGGERED, TRAPPING THE PREY.

Icebergs

Did you know that many icebergs have been around for up to 15,000 years? Their size is something to be reckoned with, too. Many northern hemisphere icebergs weigh literally millions of tonnes, and they contain enough water to supply 150,000 people—for a whole year.

North of the equator, around 40,000 icebergs 'calve' or break off the coast at Greenland every year, and then start drifting towards Canada's Newfoundland. They can drift up to 4,000 kilometres or 2,485 miles south; unusual iceberg sightings have been made from the coasts of Ireland and even Bermuda. The largest iceberg ever spotted and recorded in the Northern Hemisphere was 8.07 miles long, and 3.7 miles wide—which is nearly 30 square miles. Its weight was said to be in excess of nine billion tonnes and it contained enough water for every single person in the whole world to drink a litre a day for over four years.

The Southern Hemisphere has the largest icebergs of all. In 1955 an iceberg was spotted about 150 miles west of Scott Island, inside the Antarctic Circle. It was reported to be 60 miles wide by 208 miles long, or about 12,000 square miles or 31,000 square kilometres.

You may ask yourself, "If icebergs are so big, why do they not just sink?"—well, the reason that icebergs float is that ice has a density of around 900 kilograms per cubic metre, whereas seawater has a density of around 1,025 kilograms per cubic metre. The ratios of these two densities tell us that seven-eighths of an iceberg must be below the water line.

Iceberg water is now even being marketed to those who want to indulge in its health benefits as "the purest water in the world".

HOW DO HELICOPTERS FLY?

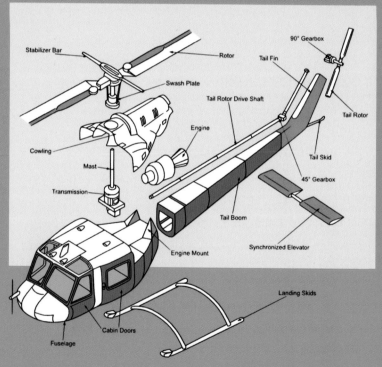

Stabilizer Bar
Rotor
90° Gearbox
Tail Fin
Swash Plate
Tail Rotor Drive Shaft
Engine
Tail Rotor
Cowling
Tail Skid
Mast
45° Gearbox
Transmission
Tail Boom
Synchronized Elevator
Engine Mount
Landing Skids
Cabin Doors
Fuselage

For people who are even a little bit apprehensive about flying in an aeroplane, the idea of getting into a helicopter is far more frightening. When a helicopter takes off–and they are also a lot smaller and more fragile-looking than planes–well, the whole process just looks at first glance to be a bit more complicated and nerve-racking than when a plane takes off. Perhaps this is because it is easier for us to understand how the gathering speed of an aeroplane combines with the aerodynamic shape of its wings to 'ride' on the air sweeping underneath to achieve take-off.

The brave person who designed, built and rode the first helicopter as we know them today was a Russian aircraft pioneer called Igor Sikorsky. He achieved lift-off in the first fully controllable single rotor/tail rotor helicopter in 1939, right at the beginning of the Second World War.

When Sikorsky started out, his first priority was to get the helicopter to lift. This is relatively straightforward, as the easiest way to get 'straight-up' lift is through continuous rotary motion of the blades, which are shaped like the wings of a plane and work on exactly the same principle. On that first experimental 'flight' in September 1939, the best Sikorsky could manage was to lift the helicopter off the ground and then set it down again a few times. The craft vibrated excessively, and according to eyewitnesses, Sikorsky was a complete blur as he sat at the controls of the open craft in his topcoat and fedora hat to protect him from the cold. The helicopter had to be kept safe with wires tethering it to weights on the ground.

Within a couple of months of the first flight, he managed to make the craft hop into the air for a minute or two–then in December 1939, a gust of wind caught the craft from behind and tipped it onto the ground, smashing the rotor blades. The mechanics began to despair, and called the machine "Igor's nightmare".

But Sikorsky kept at it, and on 13 May 1940 the first 'free flight' happened. By this time he had worked out how to fully solve the problem of having spinning rotor blades attached to a shaft, which make the body of a craft want to spin like crazy in the opposite direction to the blades: he provided another smaller rotating blade to the tail, at right angles to the main rotor, whose sideways thrust counteracted the body's desire to spin. To change direction, the angle of the main rotor and tail rotors were made adjustable, and a more powerful engine was also used.

By the middle of 1940, a 15 minute flight time was achieved; and despite a description by another test-flight pilot of it being "like a bucking bronco", the US Army Air Corps was impressed enough to grant a contract to Sikorsky so he could develop a more refined experimental helicopter. 18 different versions followed until 6 May 1941, when the longest flight time to date was achieved at one hour, 32 minutes and 26 seconds.

By the end of the Second World War, more than 400 Sikorsky helicopters had been produced for the US Army.

New!

Aluminium

What comes to mind when you think about aluminium? Cooking foil. Lightness?

Believe it or not, aluminium makes up about eight per cent of the composition of the earth's crust— which when you think about it, is really an awful lot of aluminum.

Aluminium is a very versatile material; it resists corrosion, is a good heat insulator, conducts electricity efficiently and most of all, compared to other metals, it is incredibly light. It is essential in the aerospace, packing and electrical industries, and is used for many cooking utensils. Powdered aluminium is used in paints, and in rocket fuel.

With such a variety of uses, it is perhaps surprising to learn that aluminium was only discovered during the nineteenth century. The reason for this is the metal is never found alone, it is always in ores containing another compound. The substance containing the most aluminium is a mineral called boxite, which is almost half aluminium.

Intelligence Test

Have a go at this intelligence test. According to Mensa, the 'High IQ Society', if you get 19 or more of these 33 questions correct, you are a proper 'genius'. Apparently only two Mensa members achieved full marks.

You have to work out what pattern the letters are referring to.

For example:

24 H in a D = 24 Hours in a Day

Scoring:

1–5: average intelligence
6–11: somewhat intelligent
12–18: intelligent
19–33: genius
See how many you get (no cheating now!)

1.	26 L of the A
2.	7 D of the W
3.	7 W of the W
4.	12 S of the Z
5.	66 B of the B
6.	52 C in a P (WJs)
7.	13 S in the USF
8.	18 H on a G C
9.	39 B of the O T
10.	5 T on a F

11.	90 D in a R A
12.	3 B M (S H T R)
13.	32 is the T in D F at which W F
14.	15 P in a R T
15.	3 W on a T
16.	100 C in a R
17.	11 P in a F (S) T
18.	12 M in a Y
19.	13 = UFS
20.	8 T on a O
21.	29 D in F in a L Y
22.	27 B in the N T
23.	365 D in a Y
24.	13 L in a B D
25.	52 W in a Y
26.	9 L of a C
27.	60 M in a H
28.	23 P of C in the H B
29.	64 S on a C B
30.	9 P in S A
31.	6 B to an O in C
32.	1000 Y in a M
33.	15 M on a D M C

Answers are at
the end of the
book on page
172/173

Fig. 2.—Sting of Worker-bee (*Apis mellifica*).
(After Kraepelin):

122

BEE AND WASP STINGS

Bees work hard. A single average beehive can produce around 40 pounds of honey per year. With the right conditions, this can increase to around 100 pounds. But an individual worker bee will only produce around one twelfth of a teaspoon of honey during its six week life, and to produce that honey he will quite literally work himself to death.

Bees have to protect their hives, and will sting you if you get too near and they sense their hive is threatened. However more often than not, when it comes to being stung, the culprit will be a wasp rather than a bee. Wasps are generally more aggressive, and whereas bees usually stick to feeding on the nectar and pollen from flowers, wasps are scavengers, who will hover around gatherings of people in search of food.

If a bee stings you, it fires a barbed stinger into your skin, which takes with it part of the bee's entrails and cannot be retracted. The bee has to leave both stinger and entrails behind, and as a result, it dies shortly afterwards. Wasps, on the other hand, do not have large barbs on their stingers, but serrated edges which mean their stingers can be injected into your skin and then retracted intact. The wasp is then free to move on to another target.

Self-preservation is important to all species, which is why bees are less likely

to use their sting–they know they will die. That is why you are far more likely to be stung by a wasp than a bee.

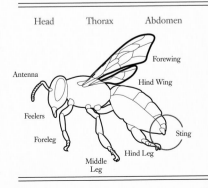

Head   Thorax   Abdomen

Forewing

Antenna

Hind Wing

Feelers

Foreleg

Sting

Hind Leg

Middle Leg

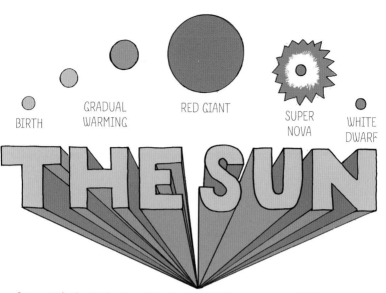

BIRTH   GRADUAL   RED GIANT   SUPER   WHITE
         WARMING   NOVA   DWARF

THE SUN

Our sun is by far the largest object in the whole of our solar system, containing around 99.8 per cent of the total mass of all the planets and their associated moons. All the other planets and moons only have around 0.2 per cent, which is virtually nothing in comparison; this gives you an idea of just how huge the sun really is. If you take the whole of the galaxy, it is said that our sun falls into the top ten per cent of every star in terms of size.

So what is this huge fiery ball actually made of? It is mostly gas—around 70 per cent hydrogen and 28 per cent helium—and the remaining two per cent are metals. This hydrogen-helium combination is in a constant state of change as the sun converts hydrogen to helium by nuclear fusion reactions, creating power in the form of gamma rays.

The sun is very gradually increasing its output, and since its beginning around 4.5 billion years ago its intensity has grown by around 40 per cent. Scientists reckon that this has used up almost half of its power, and that it has around five billion years left.

Have you ever noticed that the sun appears to be the same size as the moon when you look at it from earth? This is an extraordinary mathematical coincidence, because the sun is about 93 million miles away from the earth and the moon is only about 239,000 miles away. The massive distance away set against the massive difference in size makes both of them look the same size from earth; you can see this for yourself when you see pictures of solar eclipses, when the moon comes directly between the earth and the sun. Visually, the moon covers the sun almost exactly.

INSIDE THE SUN

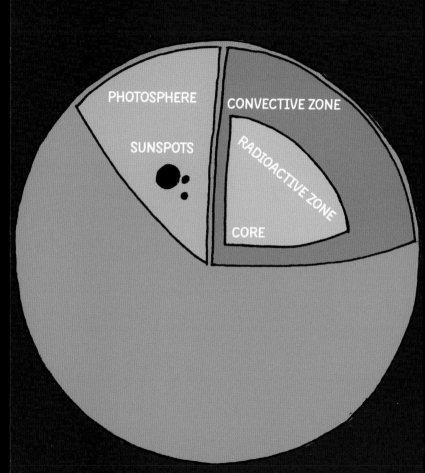

PHOTOSPHERE

CONVECTIVE ZONE

SUNSPOTS

RADIOACTIVE ZONE

CORE

Why does chrome rust on your bike but not in your bathroom?

Many bike owners love to cover their scooters or motorbikes with chrome accessories, such as multiple chrome mirrors, chrome side panels and chromed mudguards and glove-boxes. Along with the great investment in all these accessories, the owners also have to worry about stopping everything from rusting, which can happen a lot in rainy climates. But why is it that the chrome taps in your bathroom–which are exposed to as much water as anything could be–do not rust, and yet frequent rain showers will have the opposite effect on your bike, and in time, cause patches of rust to appear?

Rust, or iron oxide, is actually a separate compound from metal, and it comes about when some metals get wet and are then exposed to the elements. Once water molecules–especially rain molecules, which contain more acid than tap water–have been there for a while, they start to react with the carbon dioxide that is in the air, and together they form carbonic acid. Metals are susceptible to weakening by the chemical bonds of this acid, and they start to dissolve and wear away. At the same time, the water molecules themselves break down into hydrogen and oxygen. Whilst the hydrogen molecules are released into the air, the oxygen molecules combine with the dissolving metal to form this new compound: rust.

However, chrome is a metal that does not rust on its own; the rust you may see on chrome is in fact from corrosion of the underlying metal that is giving structural resilience, and not from corrosion of the chrome itself. Steel and iron are metals whose structural properties make them appropriate for bikes and cars, however, they are also very susceptible to rust; so they have to be very thoroughly prepared, normally in the form of copper or nickel plating, before being finished with a chrome plate layer. Much of the rust we see on chrome is the result of insufficient copper or nickel plating prior to the chrome plating process. In time, this leads to cracking and exposure of the underlying iron or steel to moisture in the air, and therefore to rust problems. Cracking is more likely to occur on bikes and cars, because they experience more mechanical stressing.

Because bathroom fittings will be constantly exposed to water, their manufacturers use materials which are far less likely to rust. They also use extremely thorough processes in bonding the chrome plating to the underlying metal, which is usually brass–an alloy of copper and zinc–and does not rust at all.

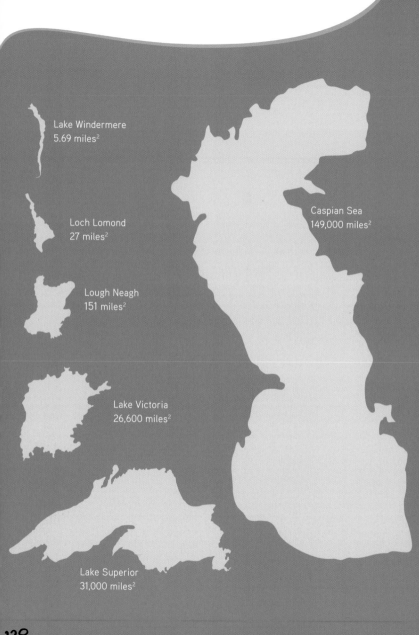

Lake Windermere
5.69 miles²

Loch Lomond
27 miles²

Lough Neagh
151 miles²

Caspian Sea
149,000 miles²

Lake Victoria
26,600 miles²

Lake Superior
31,000 miles²

Lakes

The British are very proud of their lakes, such as the romantic Lake Windermere in the Lake District, which is 5.69 square miles, and Loch Lomond in Scotland, which is 27 square miles, both of which may seem enormous to anyone who has not seen any of the world's Great Lakes. However, the honour of largest lake in the UK goes to Lough Neagh in Northern Ireland, which is about 151 square miles. You could fit Lake Windermere into Lough Neagh 26 and a half times!

As far as the largest lake in the world goes, this is the Caspian Sea, which is not a sea at all because it has no outflows and is simply an enormous lake. It borders with five countries: Azerbaijan, Russia, Kazakhstan, Turkmenistan and Iran, and is the biggest lake on our planet, at 149,200 square miles in area. Lake Windermere would fit in here just over 26,221 times.

After the Caspian Sea in size, comes Lake Superior, on the border between Canada and the US. It is over 31,000 square miles, and is considered to be the largest of the Great Lakes by those people who count Lake Michigan and Lake Huron as two separate lakes. 5,448 Lake Windermere could fit into Lake Superior.

Next comes Lake Victoria in Tanzania, East Africa. The intrepid Scottish explorer Dr David Livingstone was the first European to set eyes on Lake Victoria in 1858, when he was looking for the source of the Nile; he named it in honour of Queen Victoria. Windermere still pales in comparison, and would fit in here very nearly 4,715 times.

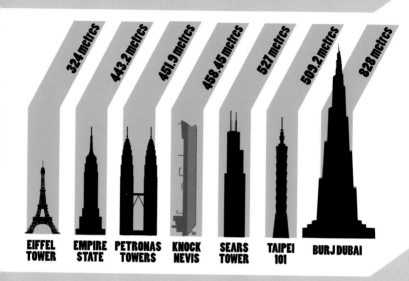

324 metres · 443.2 metres · 451.9 metres · 458.45 metres · 527 metres · 509.2 metres · 828 metres

| EIFFEL TOWER | EMPIRE STATE | PETRONAS TOWERS | KNOCK NEVIS | SEARS TOWER | TAIPEI 101 | BURJ DUBAI |

SUPER TANKERS

BRIDGE · OIL TANKS · EMPTY · FUEL TANK · ENGINE ROOM · PUMP ROOM · DOUBLE HULL

You may never have seen a supertanker up close, because they are too big to fit into ports and have to take their cargo on board at offshore platforms. They usually off-load their cargo by pumping the oil into much smaller tankers off the coast at what are called "lightering points".

These days, the word 'supertanker' is informally used to describe carriers with a maximum load weight of more than 250,000 tonnes. Many supertankers are capable of carrying around two million barrels of oil, but there are also those that can carry double that volume.

- One barrel of oil = 42 US gallons
- An average supertanker can carry about 84 million US gallons
- The biggest supertankers can carry about 170 million US gallons

Many supertankers weigh about the same as the maximum load they can carry, yet can still travel at up to 18 miles per hour when fully loaded at sea. They can be almost a quarter of a mile in length, and as the ships are split into several holding tanks, each tank can be the size of a cathedral.

Huge ship size can be a disadvantage in terms of stopping and turning around; a fully loaded supertanker takes around 14 minutes to stop, over 1.8 miles. Its turning diameter is almost 1.2 miles.

The main reason why these ships are so enormous is both to supply oil as efficiently as possible and to get as much profit as possible out of each one. They cost tens of millions of dollars each, and are therefore a colossal investment; but with high oil prices, a supertanker carrying crude oil from Saudi Arabia to the east coast of North America can pay for itself after about four successful return journeys. Only a couple of pennies per gallon are added for delivery costs.

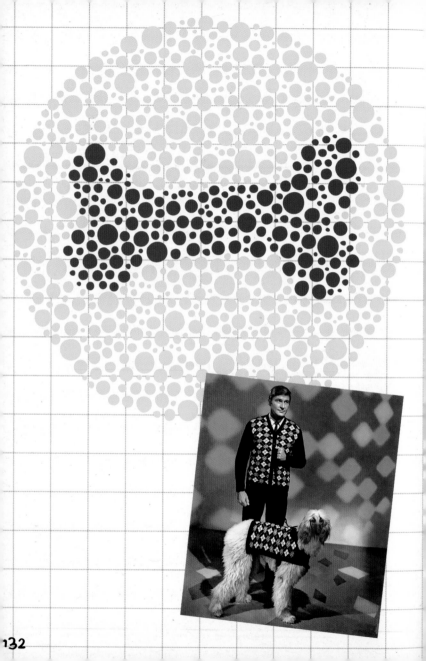

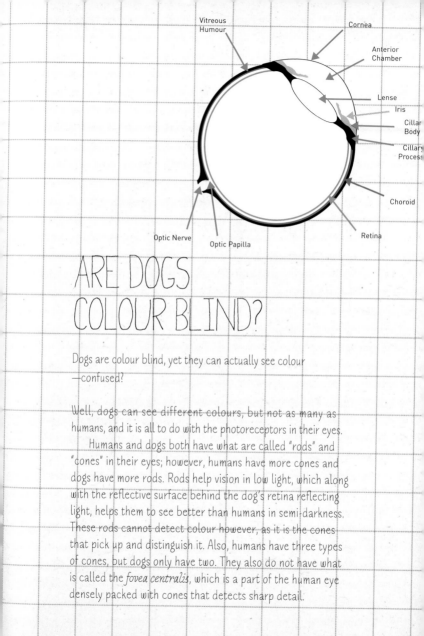

Vitreous Humour

Cornea

Anterior Chamber

Lense

Iris

Cillar Body

Cillary Process

Choroid

Retina

Optic Nerve

Optic Papilla

ARE DOGS COLOUR BLIND?

Dogs are colour blind, yet they can actually see colour —confused?

Well, dogs can see different colours, but not as many as humans, and it is all to do with the photoreceptors in their eyes.

Humans and dogs both have what are called "rods" and "cones" in their eyes; however, humans have more cones and dogs have more rods. Rods help vision in low light, which along with the reflective surface behind the dog's retina reflecting light, helps them to see better than humans in semi-darkness. These rods cannot detect colour however, as it is the cones that pick up and distinguish it. Also, humans have three types of cones, but dogs only have two. They also do not have what is called the *fovea centralis*, which is a part of the human eye densely packed with cones that detects sharp detail.

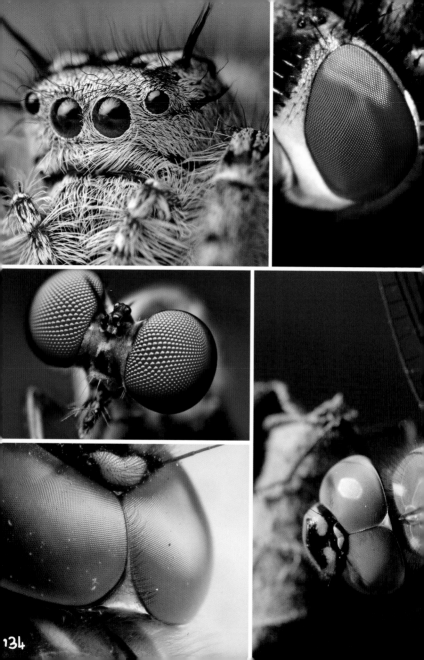

BUG EYES

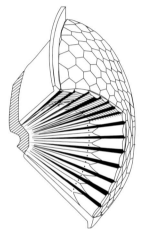

Spiders—who are not in fact insects, but *arachnids*—mostly have eight eyes. Depending on the species, they usually have some eyes on top of their head, and others at the front, but even with all those eyes, their eyesight is not particularly good. They make up for this bad eyesight with a tremendous sensitivity to vibration, usually through their webs.

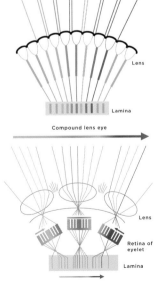

Compound eye
Lens
Lamina
Compound lens eye
Lens
Retina of eyelet
Lamina

Many insects have what are called compound eyes. Compound eyes are in fact two large eyes, which are made up of thousands of tiny individual eyes. Flies have both two compound eyes and three regular or 'simple' eyes, all working together, allowing them to see in every direction. It is thought that the two compound eyes, one on each side of its head, see close detail. The three simple eyes sit in a triangular formation between the compound eyes, and they help the fly to detect movement. It appears that nobody has ever been able to count the number of tiny eyes within a compound eye, so we may simply have to accept the figure of "a few thousand eyes".

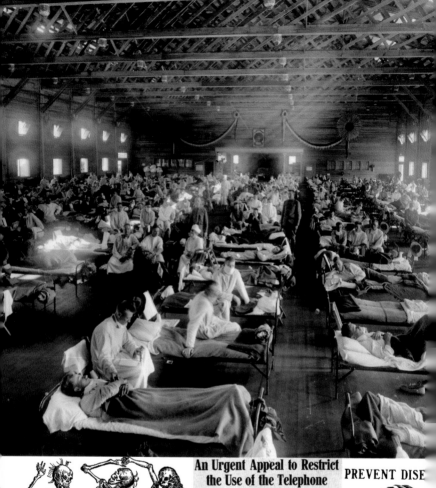

An Urgent Appeal to Restrict the Use of the Telephone

THE large number of operators now absent because of illness makes it necessary for us to appeal to our patrons to restrict the use of the telephone.

The thanks of the community are due to those patrons who have already restricted the use of the telephone, thus helping the service of war industries, hospitals and stricken homes in the city.

The Pacific Telephone and Telegraph Company

THE 1918 FLU PANDEMIC

Did you know that the flu pandemic of 1918 is thought to have infected around half of the world's population of that time? Around one billion people caught it, and around 50 million people died.

We think nothing of switching on the television or the Internet for instant news updates, or reading stories from around the world in newspapers every day, but in 1918 there were no rapid warnings for anything. This virus spread quickly and without any warning. It is still not known for sure exactly where it began, but the first known recorded case was during March 1918, at a place called Camp Fuston in Kansas. That said, it is also thought that the virus could have been around field hospitals in France during the First World War as early as 1917.

In Britain alone, the pandemic claimed the lives of 250,000 people; perhaps not surprising, when considering the limited medical advice available at the time that suggested such measures as boiling handkerchiefs and gargling with salt water.

Flu infections usually infect the nasal passages, but the major difference between this and other viruses was that this time it was reaching the lungs, leading to pneumonia. More people were killed from the 1918 flu pandemic than during any other outbreak of disease in recorded history, including the Black Death during the Middle Ages.

138

DISHWASHERS

Many of us have had conversations at some point about whether dishwashers are worth having. People may say things like, "dishwashers are very wasteful with water" or "they do not clean things properly," or even, "dishwashers are for lazy people".

People having these conversations in around 1850 might have had a point, because the only device for washing dishes available then was a device made of wood and cranked by hand, with water being sprayed onto the dishes. Speed and reliability improved when machines with permanent plumbing came about in the 1920s; but electric drying was not in operation until 1940.

Efficiency improved, and the 1950s saw their popularity grow steadily until the 1970s, when the machines became a commonplace sight in many kitchens. These models still used up to around 15 gallons of water per cycle, however; which is roughly the same as doing the dishes after a whole meal by hand, including pots and pans—and they also used a lot of electricity in comparison to washing up.

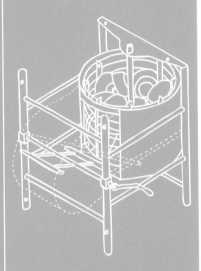

Nowadays, dishwashers use about six to eight gallons of water, which is without doubt more efficient. In terms of energy use, the hot water can now be heated in the dishwasher itself, rather than in the household hot water heater, where much of the heat can get lost in transit. They also only use as much water as is needed.

140

Where Do Place Names Come From?

Please Drive Carefully.

Have you ever wondered where city, town and village names came from? They are not simply chosen at random. Every place name has some kind of clue in it, and the study of place names is known as "toponymy".

Some places have been named after hometowns of the people who founded the place; such as Birmingham in Alabama, USA, which is named after Birmingham in England, one of the major industrial cities there. The same goes for Brighton in New Zealand, named after the Victorian spa town on the southern English coast.

The linguistic origins of many Anglo-Saxon place names often lie in an Old English, Gaelic, or Norse name for a natural landscape feature at or near the place in question. For example, the old word for a shallow crossing over a river or a stretch of water is "ford"; places such as Bradford, Ashford, Stratford and Chandler's Ford will be called so because their original settlers came there to be near the shallow water, probably during the times before building bridges was as common as it is now.

Other endings are simply describing the size and type of the original settlement. Places ending in the letters "-by", including Whitby, Wetherby, and Selby, have their origin in the Danish word "byr", which means settlement or village. Then there are the towns and villages ending in the letters "-thorpe", such as Scunthorpe, Mablethorpe, Goldthorpe. "Thorpe" is the Danish word for "hamlet". Not surprisingly, many places with names ending in the letters "by" and "thorpe" are on or near the East coast of England, which is closest to Scandanavia, from where the Vikings came.

Continued...

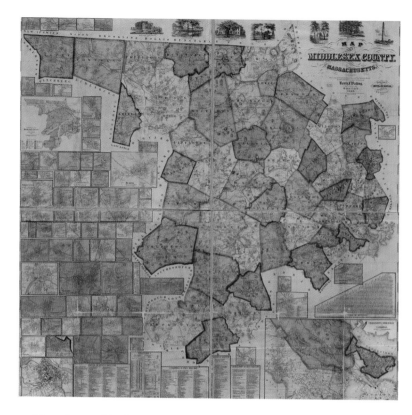

Many places end in "-ham"; a great many are cities, such as Birmingham, Nottingham and Durham. "Ham" originally meant "homestead"; so in other words, Birmingham could originally have been just a single house or farm. Then there is the ending "-ton", such as Wolverhampton, Southampton and Northampton. The old English word "ton" meant an enclosure or estate.

You may notice patterns within the names of places in a particular area; these can sometimes help you to imagine what

the area used to be like, hundreds of years ago. There is a tight concentration of towns and villages ending with these letters "ley" within a fairly small area of West Yorkshire in the North of England. "Ley" derives from "leah", an Old English word meaning "woodland clearing"–so we know just from this that at one time the area was very densely forested. There's Bingley, Keighley, Morley, Ilkley, Otley, Guiseley, and Calverley, to name just a few; and they are all so close together, that it makes you wonder whether hundreds

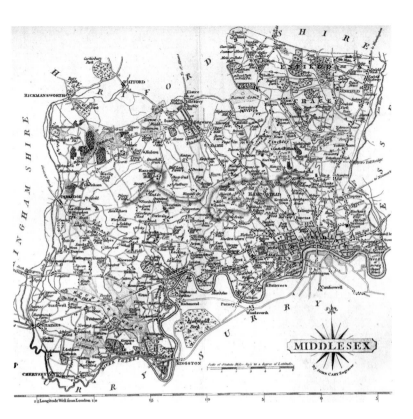

of years ago in that part of the world there might have been members of a single large family who extended their territory outward, making clearings in the woodland, claiming these for themselves and naming them accordingly.

The Romans also left their mark on place names during their occupation of the British Isles, despite keeping many of the original Anglo-Saxon names. The Latin word "castra", which means military camp or castle, evolved into "-chester" and "-caster". From this we now have the names Manchester, Chester, Rochester, Doncaster and so on. The Latin word "strata" means straight road, and evolved into "strat". Stratford incorporates this word; we could infer that at one time, Stratford was a place with a straight road and a shallow crossing over a river. It is also thought that the word "street" came from this Latin word 'strata'.

Most people have heard of the sinking of the *Titanic*, and know that it was a so-called "unsinkable" ship that struck an iceberg in the north Atlantic, resulting in a huge loss of life.

Around 1,500 people died when the *Titanic* sank. There have been lots of books written on the subject, and various films and documentaries, to the point where many assume that the sinking of the *Titanic* must have been the biggest loss of life in maritime history. But it was not; there have been other sea disasters where far more people died.

The *Wilhelm Gustloff* was a German ship designed to hold 1,800 passengers; but on 30 January 1945 it was overloaded with over 10,000 German refugees trying to escape from the Soviet Army. Of these 10,000 refugees, around 4,000 are said to have been children and youths. It was torpedoed by a Russian S-13 submarine and around 9,000 people were killed–that is six times more deaths than the *Titanic*. And the *Goya*, which was involved in the same operation, went down with the loss of between 6,000 and 7,000 lives. That is four to five times more deaths than the *Titanic*.

It is quite surprising to see the numbers of people killed in the sinking of other ships that many of us have never heard of.

Name of ship	What happened	Where	When	Number killed
Wilhelm Gustloff	German transport ship torpedoed by a Russian submarine	Baltic Sea	1945	9,000
Goya	German transport ship torpedoed by a Russian submarine	Baltic Sea	1945	6,000–7,000
Dona Paz	Philippines passenger ferry collided with the Vector, a tanker	Tablas Strait, South China Sea	1987	4,375 (combined deaths on Dona Paz and Vector)
RMS Titanic	Ocean liner struck an iceberg on her maiden voyage	North Atlantic	1912	1,500
SS Sultana	River steamer whose boilers exploded	Mississippi River	1865	1,450
RMS Lusitania	British Liner torpedoed by a German submarine	Irish Sea	1915	1,198
Toya Maru	Japanese passenger ferry sunk in a typhoon	Pacific Ocean	1954	1,172
Empress of Ireland	Ocean liner collided with a Norwegian coal freighter	St Lawrence River, Canada	1914	1,024
General Slocum	Paddle steamer caught fire	New York's East River	1914	1,021

AS BLIND AS A BAT?

Bats are often associated with spookiness, witches, Halloween and vampires. They are regarded as furry flying rats that hide in church belfries, only coming out at night and unable to see where they are going.

But the facts are that all bats have eyes, can see, and are not related to rats. There are more than 1,000 known species of bats, more than any other flying mammal in the world. Generally speaking, bats can be split into two categories: fruit-eating bats, and insect-eating bats. There are also vampire bats, which feed on the blood of cattle and other large animals.

Most fruit-eating bats have very good eyesight, and some of them have quite large eyes, as they have to be able to see in order to locate the trees growing the type of fruit they want to eat. Insect-eating bats, however, often live and feed in caves and very dark places, so their eyesight is not very good. They eat huge numbers of mosquitoes and other insects, making it possible in certain parts of the world for people to go outdoors in the summer.

Bats are not nearly as dependent on their eyes as humans are, because they also use what is called "echolocation"—or sound waves—to find their way around. They make a very high-pitched range of sounds out of their mouth and sometimes their nose, most of which are beyond the range of the human ear. Then, with their exceptionally good hearing, they listen for the echo to return from a nearby object, which could be the floor, ceiling, a tree, or even a swarm of insects. Bearing in mind that some bats can fly as fast as 60 miles per hour, this all happens in milliseconds and it is, in fact, an extremely sophisticated rapid response radar.

Some insect-eating bats in certain cave environments are so efficient they can create a food source through their own excrement. The waste they excrete is eaten by a tiny organism, which in turn is eaten by a maggot. This maggot is then eaten by a beetle, which is then eaten by a bat. Then, the cycle starts all over again, giving the bat a continuous source of food.

Bats vary hugely in size; the smallest bats are only about the size of a hornet, but the largest ones— flying fox bats—can have a wing span of 1.5 metres.

Sidenats grama
Bouteloua curtipendula

Sand dropseed
Sporobolus cryptandrus

Sand lovegrass
Eragrostis trichodes

Buffalograss
Buchloe dactyloides

Needle and thread
Hesperostipa comata

Green needlegrass
Nassella viridula

Alkali sacaton
Sporobolus airoides

Galleta
Hilaria jamesii

Big bluestem
Andropogon gerardii

Western wheatgrass
Pascopyrum smithii

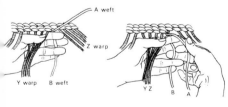

A weft

Z warp

Y warp   B weft

Y Z   B   A

HOW'YA TRADE COUSIN?

148

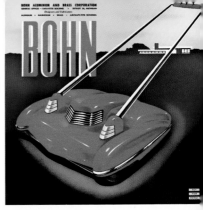

Grass
The Green Stuff

Indiangrass
Schizachyrium scoparium

Basketdrips
Cenna cinerous

Blue grama
Bouteloua gracilis

Little bluestem
Schizachyrium scoparium

Grass is one of the most versatile life forms on earth. The technical term for grass is graminoids, and there are literally thousands of types of grass, without which our planet would grind to a halt. They include the obvious lawn grasses used in gardens and sports fields, but also include bamboos, cereals, papyrus, rice and even water chestnuts, of the kind found in Chinese cooking. Grasses supply the majority of food crops for us, as well as paper, roofing, fuel, clothes—cotton is a species of grass—insulation, furniture, and many alcoholic drinks. We simply could not get by without grass.

Many animals also depend on grasses for their very existence, including cows, sheep, rabbits, goats, camels, deer, giraffes and horses. There are grass-eating insects such as caterpillars and grasshoppers, which are eaten in turn by birds, reptiles and rodents. Even sea grass is eaten by some fish.

In many places, grass is a great status symbol. Along certain streets you will see what appears to be a competition in order to see "who has the best lawn". Although they may only be there to look at, many people take their lawns very seriously indeed. A good lawn can actually make the property significantly more desirable, increasing its value by up to 11 per cent.

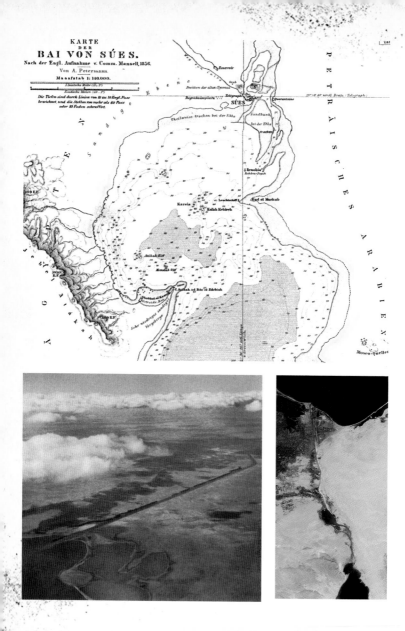

KARTE
DER
BAI VON SÚES.

Nach der Engl. Aufnahme v. Comm. Mansell, 1856.

Von A. Petermann.

Maasstab 1: 140.000.

Die Tiefen sind durch Linien von 10 zu 10 Engl. Fuss bezeichnet, und die Stellen von mehr als 60 Fuss oder 10 Faden schraffirt.

150

THE SUEZ
CANAL

The Suez Canal connects the Mediterranean Sea to the Red Sea, and it is a vital and highly valued route for the transportation of goods between Europe and Asia–with a turbulent history since it opened in 1869.

Before its opening, ships travelling between these two parts of the world had to go all the way down, around, and up the side of the Continent of Africa, facing the challenge of the Cape of Good Hope, a treacherous piece of sea at the foot of Africa where the Atlantic Ocean meets the Indian Ocean. The other alternative was to unload cargo from ships and carry it overland, reloading at the other end, which became more and more impractical for large volumes of goods.

Ancient documents have suggested that there was a canal or connecting river as early as 1800 BC, and reliefs from an expedition in 1470 BC depict seagoing vessels travelling between the Red Sea and the Nile. Since that time there have been various reports of different connecting waterways being built, and then falling into disrepair due to the build-up of silt. Napoleon Bonaparte is reported to have been obsessed with finding the remains of a waterway during his occupation of Egypt in the 1790s, ordering a thorough scouring of the land in search of it. He also ordered a survey to examine the feasibility of building his own canal, connecting the Mediterranean with the Red Sea, but concluded that since the Mediterranean was ten metres lower than the Red Sea, locks would be required, making the project too complicated and expensive.

But the need was still there for a canal connecting Europe with Asia, to cut out the significant voyage around Africa, and on further investigation it was found that the sea level difference could in fact be accommodated

Continued...

Egyptian Premier Gamal Abdel Nasser, British Prime Minister Anthony Eden and US President Dwight Eisenhower are all 'rocking the boat' during the Suez Crisis in a political cartoon from 1956.

by shipping, and did not have as complicated implications as originally thought. So in 1858, a former French diplomat called Ferdinand de Lesseps formed The Suez Canal Company in partnership with the Egyptian government. This company was to lease the land from Egypt for 99 years, construct the canal, and then charge passage to any ship that wished to use it. The construction took almost 11 years, using 30,000 people under forced labour. It was opened for shipping on 17 November 1869 and, similar to large modern-day construction projects, came in at double the original budget.

In 1875, due to national debt, Egypt was forced to sell its share in the canal and it was purchased by the UK for four million pounds—an absolute fortune at that time. Following this purchase, the Convention of Constantinople confirmed the canal to be a neutral zone under the protection of the UK. British troops therefore had to move in

to shield the canal from attack when the Egyptian Civil War happened in 1882, and again during an Ottoman attack in 1915. In 1936, UK control over the canal was re-confirmed with the Anglo-Egyptian Treaty; but this treaty was withdrawn by the Egyptians in 1951, with the British having to gradually withdraw themselves.

Then came the infamous Suez crisis. Egypt had been warming its relations with the Soviet Union. This was perceived as a threat by the British and the Americans, so they withdrew their support for a massive project to build a vital new dam at Aswan. In 1956, President Gamal Abdal Nassar of Egypt decided to finance the Aswan Dam by nationalising the canal, and using its revenue as funds for the construction project. And in response, Britain, France and Israel planned to invade Egypt in order to re-take control of the canal.

Tensions quickly rose to boiling point. Canada was prompted to

ANGLO-FRENCH INVASION

SINAI
CAMPAIGN IN SINAI
Conquest of Sinai, 1–5 November, 1956

Between Kantara and El-Firdane—The First Vessels through the Canal.

intervene by proposing the first ever United Nations peacekeeping force. But by the time things had settled down, ships had been sunk and other damage had been done to the canal, so it had to be closed for clearance until April 1957, when it re-opened under a UN force in order to maintain its neutrality.

Trouble raised its head again in 1967, with the Arab-Israeli war. Relations had been steadily deteriorating between Egypt and Israel for some time. There were UN forces positioned as a 'cushion' between the two countries, but only on the Egyptian side of the border. When President Nassar ordered them to leave, and moved his own army forwards towards the Israeli border, Israel made a strike on Egypt—and so began the 1967 Arab-Israeli war, which is also known as the Six Day War. Following the war, the Egyptian government intentionally closed the canal for eight years, with 14 ships trapped inside for the entire time. The blockade was finally lifted

during June 1975, and the Sinai Interim Agreement, signed shortly afterwards by Egypt and Israel in Geneva, stated that the conflicts between the countries "shall not be resolved by military force but by peaceful means".

The present Suez Canal is 120 miles long and is single lane, with four passing places.

Seawater runs freely between the Mediterranean and the Red Sea, with no locks.

Ships with up to 136,000 tonnes of displacement can travel through the canal; this includes large war ships, but excludes the very large supertankers.

A ships' passage usually takes between 11 and 16 hours as low speed—eight knots—is enforced in order to reduce erosion of the banks.

Around 20,000 vessels travel through the canal every year.

The average passage price per ship is around $250,000.

PIGS

Many people regard pigs as dirty, smelly animals; the generic term for pigs is "swine", a word often used to describe someone who is dirty, bad-mannered, or pig-like in general. But they are said by many to be a very misunderstood species, and are certainly amongst the most numerous animals on the planet, with world pig population estimates ranging up to three billion.

Pigs are very intelligent animals, often considered to be cleverer than dogs. They are very quick at learning a new routine, and can be trained to do tricks such as jump through hoops, bow and stand, spin, and make word-like sounds on command; they can roll out rugs, herd sheep, and close and open cages. The fact that they like to roll around in mud is for a couple of very good reasons. First, pigs have no sweat glands, so they have to roll around in mud and water on hot days in order to stay cool; and secondly, the layer of mud protects them from flies and other insects.

Pigs are omnivores, which means they eat both animals and plants. When they live in the wild, they forage for their food, eating mostly leaves, grasses, roots, fruits and flowers. When they are kept by humans, pigs are fed mostly on cornmeal and soya bean meal; but their reputation for eating pretty much anything that is put their way is not unfounded. Leftover school dinners are often given to pigs on pig farms. There is even something called a "pig toilet", found mainly in India, which is an outhouse with a hole underneath placed over a pigsty, and the pigs live off the waste.

Pig farming can be extremely lucrative. A typical litter will contain between six and 12 piglets at a time, which is a very high return. As well as pork, pigskin is a valuable commodity and it is made into all kinds of things, including jackets, gloves, wallets and furniture.

WHO INVENTED THE FIRST CLOCK?

This question all depends on what you define as a clock. The clock, as we know it, was not simply invented one day by someone cobbling lots of wheels and cogs together. The clock actually evolved over thousands of years, and it all began with the sun. Ancient civilisations used to determine the time by observing the position of the sun in the sky by day, and the stars at night. Some people still use this method today.

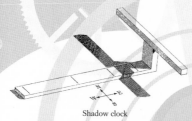

Shadow clock

The ancient Egyptians are known from around 3500 BC to have used an obelisk–a tall thin tower with a pointed top–which casts its shadow over a semi-circular area on the ground as the sun moves around it, creating a kind of clock. The shortest shadow of the day, at midday, always points in the same direction, and this point was placed at the centre of their semi-circular clock. In around 1500 BC, sundials started being used, which could be placed virtually anywhere. They were used by Greeks and Romans as well, and were especially favoured by rich people who had them placed in their gardens, enabling them to tell the time quickly rather than having to walk into town for a quick look at the local obelisk. This was a major breakthrough in timepieces, but due to their relatively small size, sundials were not very accurate.

There were also water clocks, which are thought to have been used by the Egyptians as early as 1400 BC. Initially, these were crude contraptions, relying on two containers holding water. One container was higher than the other, and as water trickled from the higher container to the lower one, markings on the container sides were observed in order to tell the time. Water clock technology moved on to

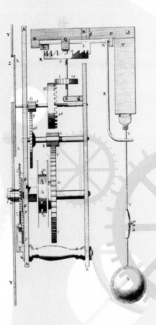

Benedictine Monk called Gerbert D'Aurillac, who would eventually become Pope Sylvester II, is credited with making the world's first pendulum clock. He was a master at mathematics and astronomy, developing working models in order to demonstrate his teachings visually to his students. He made the first ever pendulum clock, which had only one hand—to give the hour—because a minute hand had not been considered at that time.

Time marched on, and pendulum clocks became more sophisticated and accurate. Then in 1577, the Swiss mathematician and maker of astronomical instruments, Jost Bürgi, came up with the idea of adding a minute hand, which became a permanent fixture of all analogue and digital timepieces as we know them today.

the point where a float was placed in the lower tank, which was attached to a notched piece of wood that moved higher as the water level rose and this, in turn, moved a hand around a very basic clock-face. The major benefit of the water clock over the sundial was that since it did not rely on the presence of the sun, it could be used 24 hours a day and in all weather.

It was not until around the year 996 AD that another major breakthrough in timepieces was made. A French

The Mediterranean Diet

According to nutritionists, the Mediterranean diet is meant to be one of the healthiest ways of eating, because it is made up of foods that are lower in saturated fats and higher in things which have more vitamins, such as salads and fruits, olives, olive oil and oily fish, which also help to prevent heart disease.

So if you live in a European country with a Mediterranean coastline, does that mean you automatically have a Mediterranean diet? There are lots of countries with a Mediterranean coastline and most of them appear to eat different things. Let us have a look at a few of them to see how healthy they are:

Greece: Here they like yoghurt for breakfast with a little bread and honey. Lunch might be a light beef stew with bread and feta cheese. Dinner might be a meat kebab and chips, with salad on the side. Olives make for good snacks.

France: You might start off with buttery croissants for breakfast, or a pain au chocolat. Breakfast might be accompanied by a fresh coffee, or creamy hot chocolate is also popular. Lunch and dinner might start off with bread and olives, then a soup starter with bread, followed by a piece of meat or fish with fresh vegetables, and then cheese–perhaps Camembert or Brie.

Italy: Here you would start off with a creamy cappuccino and sweet pastry. Pizza, spaghetti, cannelloni, lasagna, ravioli and lots of tomatoes form a big part of lunch and dinner in Italy. Olives are also popular as a snack.

Spain: Strong coffee and churros are popular to start the day off within Spain. Churros are a kind of doughnut in the shape of a very long thick sausage, sometimes with sugar icing on top. As in France, Spanish people often have similar lunches to their dinners, and that could comprise a soup starter–perhaps a cold soup in summer–followed by a piece of meat or fish, accompanied by chips and a little salad. Especially during the hot summer months, the Spanish eat a lot of salads and fruit, plus a few olives.

Who is the healthiest amongst all these Mediterranean countries? Well, it looks like the average person eats a whole load of things other than just fish, fresh fruit and vegetables. But the common denominator in the whole Mediterranean diet seems to be: olives.

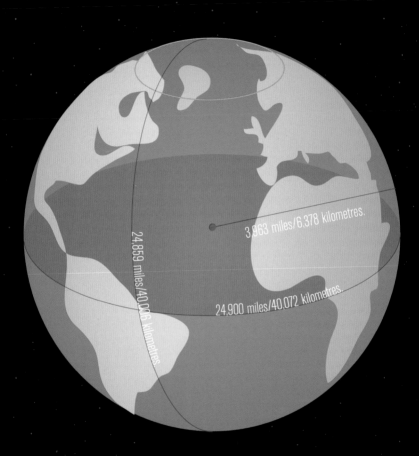

3,963 miles/6,378 kilometres.

24,900 miles/40,072 kilometres.

24,859 miles/40,006 kilometres

EARTH STATISTICS

Do you know how far it is from the surface to the centre of the earth? It is about 3,963 miles—that is 6,378 kilometres.

Do you know the distance around the earth's circumference? At the equator it is about 24,900 miles, or 40,072 kilometres. However, if you measure through the north and south poles, it is slightly less, at about 24,859 miles, or 40,006 kilometres. This is because the earth is not exactly round, and is a touch wider than it is tall.

There are all kinds of other impressive comparative statistics in relation to the Earth, such as:

● **The proportion of the thickness of the Earth's crust to the rest of its internal mass is less than the skin of an apple in proportion to its flesh.**

● **The distance from the surface to the centre of the Earth is roughly the same as the distance from Hawaii to Japan—about 4,000 miles.**

● **If you laid all 60,000 miles of blood vessels inside the average human body end to end, they would stretch around the world twice.**

● **If you took the approximately 17 billion toilet paper rolls that are produced in the US each year, end-to-end they would reach to the moon and back.**

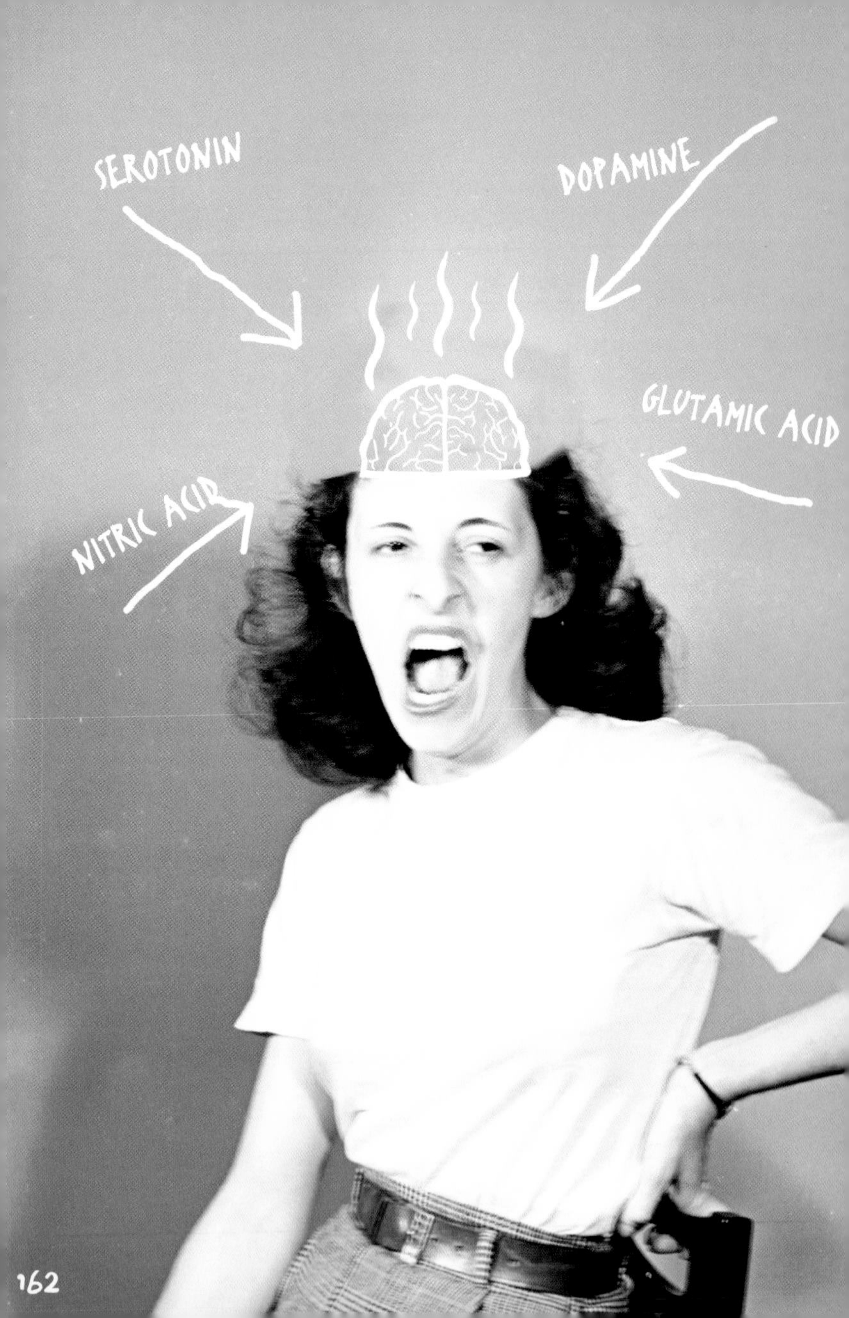

SEROTONIN

DOPAMINE

GLUTAMIC ACID

NITRIC ACID

Yawning

Yawning is a strange phenomenon. If you yawn and someone sees you, they will inevitably yawn shortly afterwards. Conversely, if you see someone yawn, it makes you yawn as well.

On a general level, yawning is associated with being tired or bored. But beyond this association, you may be surprised to learn that even today, despite great medical advances, experts cannot seem to agree on the actual causes of yawning.

There is a general consensus that yawning occurs when too much carbon dioxide is in the blood, but when it comes to what yawning is supposed to do about this, the jury is still out. Some claim that a quick injection of oxygen is needed and that a good yawn can provide this; but then some others claim that yawning may actually reduce oxygen intake, not increase it.

Muscle stretching is another theory, as is increasing general alertness. Also linked to yawning is an excessive amount of certain chemicals in the brain which are associated with emotions and appetite, such as serotonin, dopamine, glutamic acid and nitric acid. The link to emotions and moods may explain why, for example, paratroopers yawn before jumping, and dogs yawn before fighting.

Taking this theory further, it seems yawning might be the body's way of controlling brain temperature, a bit like a fan cooling a computer. Normally the body attempts to constantly control the body's temperature; heat is released through the skull, the veins in the face, or the numerous sweat glands of the forehead. Our body temperature goes up during stressful moments, in the midst of a migraine, when we are sleep deprived, or when we are just plain drowsy. Many experts now think that yawning may take over to cool down our brains during those times when our normal thermal regulation processes are not efficient enough.

One thing that all the experts seem to agree on, however, is that yawning is contagious—have you yawned yourself whilst reading this?

POST-MORTEMS

Post-mortems, or autopsies, are carried out when someone dies suddenly, violently or under strange circumstances. They are also carried out if someone dies from a rapid-onset disease, where the findings could aid medical science. of the deceased. In very extreme circumstances, such as a public health emergency, the Secretary of State for Health can override the wishes of the next of kin and order a post-mortem. Also, in certain circumstances, if a post-mortem

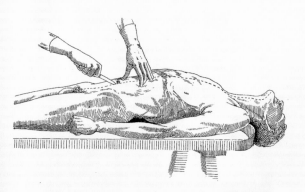

Either a coroner will order a post-mortem, or a hospital will request it. The difference is that if a coroner orders a post-mortem it must take place by law, even if the next of kin disagrees. If, however, a hospital requests a post-mortem, the hospital must secure written permission from the next of kin is not requested by a hospital, the relatives of the deceased can request one in order to learn more about the reasons why their loved one died.

Performed by pathologists–doctors trained in the art of the diagnosis of disease and the identification of the cause of death–the procedures vary in a

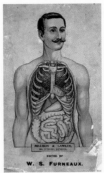

W. S. FURNEAUX.

post-mortem from country to country, and can also vary in their degree of exploration, from the examination of one single organ, such as the heart, to a total examination.

The procedure begins with a complete external examination where the weight and height of the deceased are recorded together with any markings, such as wounds, scars, tattoos, etc.. The internal examination then begins, sometimes with a Y shaped cut from both shoulders running down the front of the chest, meeting at the sternum and then down to the pubic bone; or a T-shaped cut, from the tip of both shoulders in a horizontal line across the area of the collarbone and from its centre, down to the pubic bone. Once the initial cuts have been made, the skin and tissue are lifted to expose the ribcage and abdominal cavity. The front of the ribcage is then removed. At this point the chest organs, such as the heart and lungs, are revealed and can be removed, followed by the abdominal organs, such as the liver and kidneys. In order to examine the brain, an incision is made at the back of the head, and part of the skull is removed to reveal the brain.

As organs are removed from the body, they are inspected by the pathologist. Any common diseases, such as coronary artery disease and cirrhosis of the liver, are often immediately evident. Individual organs may be dissected further in order to reveal such things as tumours, and small samples are often taken for further microscopic examination. Sometimes post-mortems can reveal a misdiagnosis. Once the post-mortem is finished, the incisions are sewn back up.

It is believed that post-mortems were carried out by the ancient Greeks, and the ancient Egyptians were removing internal body parts around 3000 BC as part of the mummification process. Julius Caesar had an autopsy carried out on him in 44 BC, at which physicians apparently established that the second stab wound on his body was the fatal one in his assassinations. Since that time, the practice has been adopted by many countries and civilisations, not least for the advancement of anatomical science.

Fathoms knots AND nautical miles

SIX FEET = ONE FATHOM

15 FATHOMS(30YARDS) = ONE SHACKLE

6,080 FEET (1,853.18 METRES) = ONE NAUTICAL MILE

6,076 FEET (1,852 METRES) = ONE 'INTERNATIONAL' NAUTICAL MILE

Most of us have heard of these nautical terms, but may not nessessarily know what they mean. They originate from long before our metric times to the old seafaring days and were very cleverly devised.

Fathoms are used to measure the depth of water, and have been around since before the 1600s. It is thought that the original measurement came from measuring the length of a man's arms when stretched out horizontally, from fingertip to fingertip—about six feet. The US Hydrographic Office still uses feet and fathoms to measure depth.

The knot is used for measuring speed, and can be defined as one nautical mile per hour. Sailors used to stand at the back of a ship, and throw a knotted rope with a shaped log tied at the end of it over into the water. The number of knots in the cable pulled over the side into the water within a given time—usually 30 seconds—determined the speed of the vessel in knots.

Nautical miles are the seafarers' way of measuring distance, and are quite different from the miles we use on land. Originally, they were based on the circumference of the world at the equator, which has 360 degrees of longitude around it. Each one of these 360 degrees is then split into 60 so-called minutes. So on that basis— 360 x 60—there are 21,600 minutes of longitude around the earth. This was how the original nautical mile came into being, with one minute of longitude at the equator making one nautical mile, about 6,080 feet.

These old nautical miles could also be broken down into "shackles". A shackle is a D-shaped piece of metal which connects lengths of cable together; the lengths themselves came to be known as shackles, and ships were usually equipped with 12 shackles of bower cable. When dropping anchor, the sailors could judge the water depth by the number of shackles of rope pulled over the side by the anchor.

In 1954, it was abandoned in the US in favour of the international nautical mile, which is 1,852 metres, and the British Admiralty followed suit in 1970.

THE TERRACOTTA ARMY

Back in 1974, some local farmers in Shaanxi province, China, were drilling for water when they accidentally discovered underground chambers containing over 8,000 life-size warrior-style figures fashioned from terracotta clay. The Terracotta Army has caused great excitement amongst archeologists ever since.

It has emerged that China's first Emperor, Qin Shi Huang, was only 13 years old when he ordered the construction of the figures in 246 BC in readiness for his burial, so that he could rule another empire in the afterlife. He had to order this at such a young age, because it was such a massive task; it is said that around 70,000 workers were involved, and it was made all the more labour-intensive because at the Emperors' orders, every single one of these figures is completely unique. They are made with different heights and builds, with no two soldiers having the same face, and with an astonishing amount of thought and work put into the detail.

Studies tell us that around eight basic face moulds were used for the army, with clay delicately added to each one, in order to create individual facial features and expressions. Each of the life-size foot soldiers, officers, chariots and horses were painted in minute, highly coloured detail—most of which has now worn away with time—to make them as life-like as possible.

The four pits that were excavated are about seven metres deep and are very sturdily constructed. Pit One holds the main part of the foot army, consisting of approximately 8,000 figures, and is about 230 metres long. Pit Two holds the more elaborate infantry units, cavalry and chariots; and Pit Three is the command unit, holding officers and the main war chariot. Pit Four was found to be empty.

Fascinatingly, each item that makes up the figures—arms, legs, heads, and torsos—has a mark inscribed upon it, denoting which workshop it was made in, so that any defects could be traced back to the source of manufacture. So you could say that even way back in 246 BC, these people knew about quality control.

SNOTITES

Most of the time, the names given by scientists to natural phenomena are in Latin. There are thousands and thousands of examples, such as:

Galanthus nivalis	Daffodil
Lanicera caprifolium	Honeysuckle
Vacinnium mytillis	Bilberry
Forficia auricular	Earwig
Mustela erminae stabilis	Stoat

There is however one relatively recent discovery, which has been given a strikingly non-Latin name: a "snotite".

Snotites are massive colonies of living bacteria; they are slimy, mucus-like, dripping formations found in some caves, and they thrive in complete darkness. The acidic liquid that drips from a snotite can rot through your clothing. They are pretty disgusting looking things, hanging in pointed curtains, and their texture is that of slimy gunge.

They are, however, a great help to scientists exploring theories around life on other planets; the fact that snotites thrive in such inhospitable subterranean environments has prompted some to explore whether there could be similar subterranean bacterial life forms on Mars.

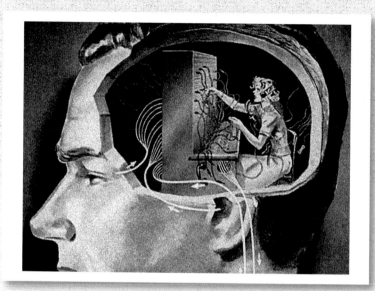

No.	Clue	Answer
1.	26 L of the A	26 letters of the alphabet
2.	7 D of the W	7 days of the week
3.	7 W of the W	7 wonders of the world
4.	12 S of the Z	12 signs of the zodiac
5.	66 B of the B	66 books of the bible
6.	52 C in a P (WJs)	52 cards in a pack (Without Jokers)
7.	13 S in the USF	13 stripes in the US flag
8.	18 H on a G C	18 holes on a golf course
9.	39 B of the O T	39 books of the old testament
10.	5 T on a F	5 toes on a foot
11.	90 D in a R A	90 degrees in a right angle
12.	3 B M (S H T R)	3 blind mice (see how they run)
13.	32 is the T in D F at which W F	32 is the temperature in degrees Fahrenheit at which water freezes
14.	15 P in a R T	15 players in a rugby team
15.	3 W on a T	3 wheels on a tricycle
16.	100 C in a R	100 cents in a rand
17.	11 P in a F (S) T	11 players in a football (soccer) team
18.	12 M in a Y	12 months in a year
19.	13 = UFS	13 = unlucky for some
20.	8 T on a O	8 tentacles on an octopus
21.	29 D in F in a L Y	29 days in February in a leap year
22.	27 B in the N T	27 books in the new testament
23.	365 D in a Y	365 days in a year
24.	13 L in a B D	13 loaves in a bakers dozen
25.	52 W in a Y	52 weeks in a year
26.	9 L of a C	9 lives of a cat
27.	60 M in a H	60 minutes in an hour
28.	23 P of C in the H B	23 pairs of chromosomes in the human body
29.	64 S on a C B	64 squares on a chess board
30.	9 P in S A	9 Provinces in South Africa
31.	6 B to an O in C	6 balls to an over in cricket
32.	1000 Y in a M	1000 years in a millennium
33.	15 M on a D M C	15 men on a dead mans chest

YOUR MARK:

/33

Credit	Page
Daily Clip Art (top right)	Front cover
James Vaughan (bottom left)	Front cover
Thomas Shahan (bottom right)	Front cover
Grand Velas RIviera Maya (left)	Back cover
Ingrid Taylar (right)	Back cover
Steven Martin (top left)	p. 5
Sue Clarke (top right)	p. 5
Jen Deering Davis (middle)	p. 5
Flydime (bottom left)	p. 5
James Vaughan (bottom right)	p. 5
David Rumsey	p. 8
From The Home and School Reference Work, Vol. 3, by The Home and School Education Society, HM Dixon	p. 14
James Vaughan	p. 17
Annie Mole	p. 19
James Vaughan	p. 24–25
James Vaughan	p. 28
Michael Studt	p. 32
James Vaughan	p. 34
Imageshack (top left)	p. 35
James Vaughan (top right and bottom)	p. 35
James Vaughan (bottom)	p. 36
Generationdynamics (top)	p. 38
Dharahn British Grammar School (bottom right)	p. 38
Reeanctor.net (top and bottom right)	p. 40
Tancrède R Duma	p. 42
Dover Publications (top)	p. 43
Nick Ehm (bottom)	p. 43
Dacosta (top left)	p. 45
Wisconsin Historical Images (top middle)	p. 45
Popular Science Monthly Vol. 4 (top right)	p. 45
Charles R Knight (bottom left)	p. 45
Martin from Tyrol (bottom middle)	p. 45
James Vaughan (bottom right)	p. 45
Daily Clip Art	p. 46
National Nuclear Security Administration, Nevada Site	p. 48
The County Clerk	p. 49
Howard Pyle	p. 50, 52
Rudolphnovk (top left) Aljawad (top right)	p. 56
Wilhelm Ritter von Haidinger	p. 57
David Hill	p. 58
James Vaughan	p. 63
Sir George W Humphreys (top)	p. 64
Ian Mansfield (bottom)	p. 64
Trey Ratcliff	p. 65
diagnostics.tumblr.com	p. 66
Sue Clark/The Home and School Education Society	p. 67
Chip Clark, Smithsonian Institution	p. 72
James Vaughan	p. 78–79
Tlyons (top left)	p. 82
NIlson FM (top right)	p. 82
Tym (bottom left)	p. 82
Marcus Trimble (bottom right)	p. 82
Thelmadatter (top left)	p. 84
Thierry (top right)	p. 84
Linz Ellinas (bottom)	p. 84
KitLKat	p. 86
Scan d'Arnaud Gaillard (left)	p. 87
Antoine-Jean Gros (bottom right)	p. 87
Allison & Allison (left)	p. 88
SSKilburn (top right)	p. 88
Maurice Michael (bottom right)	p. 88

© 2011 Black Dog Publishing Limited
and the Author.
All rights reserved.

Black Dog Publishing Limited
10A Acton Street
London
WC1X 9NG

t.   +44 (0)207 713 5097
f.   +44 (0)207 713 8682
e.   info@blackdogonline.com
w. www.blackdogonline.com

Designed by Alex Prior and Jonathan
Grey Wilson with assistance from
Estefania Hormigo, Lucy Simmons and
Grace Brothers at Black Dog Publishing.

Special thanks to Lucia Hutton.

British Library Cataloguing-in-
Publication Data.
A CIP record for this book is available
from the British Library.
ISBN   978 1 907317 50 7

Black Dog Publishing is an environmentally
responsible company. *More Interesting
Than Your Teacher* is printed on FSC
accredited paper.

architecture art design
fashion history photography
theory and things

**black dog
publishing**

www.blackdogonline.com   london uk